Streamlines: Selected Readings on Single Topics

Learning Dynamics

Marjorie Ford
Stanford University

Jon Ford
College of Alameda

Houghton Mifflin Company

Boston   New York

SPONSORING EDITOR: Jayne M. Fargnoli
SENIOR ASSOCIATE EDITOR: Janet Edmonds
EDITORIAL ASSISTANT: Terri Teleen
ASSOCIATE PROJECT EDITOR: Rebecca Bennett
ASSOCIATE PRODUCTION COORDINATOR: Deborah Frydman
SENIOR MANUFACTURING COORDINATOR: Marie Barnes

COVER DESIGNER: Diana Coe

 As part of Houghton Mifflin's ongoing commitment to the environment, this text has been printed on recycled paper.

Acknowledgments

Maya Angelou, "Graduation" from *I Know Why The Caged Bird Sings*. Copyright © 1969 and renewed 1997 by Maya Angelou. Reprinted by permission of Random House, Inc.

Howard Gardner, "In a Nutshell" from *Multiple Intelligences*. Copyright © 1993 by Howard Gardner. Reprinted by permission of BasicBooks, a division of HarperCollins Publishers, Inc.

E. D. Hirsch, "The Common School and the Common Good" from *The Schools We Need and Why We Don't Have Them*. Copyright © 1995 by Doubleday, a division of Bantam Doubleday Dell Publishing Group. Used by permission of Doubleday, a division of Bantam Doubleday Dell Publishing Group, Inc.

Acknowledgments continue on p. 117, which constitutes an extension of the copyright page.

Printed in the U.S.A.

Library of Congress Catalog Card Number: 97-72471
ISBN: 0-395-86798-3

23456789—CS—01 00 99 98

CONTENTS

A series of six books on intriguing, relevant topics, *Streamlines: Selected Readings on Single Topics* are an innovation among composition textbooks for college writing courses. Designed to encourage creativity, critical thinking, and research in writing classrooms, the series presents a range of texts to choose from: classic and contemporary essays, literature, journalistic writing, research-based writing, and student essays. The books can be used individually or in combination. Each book allows instructors to delve deeply into single topics—Learning, Health, Relationships, the Natural World, Work, and Mass Culture and Electronic Media—while allowing for a variety of teaching approaches. Some instructors may assign one or two of the books in addition to readings in a general purpose reader and a rhetoric/handbook to provide strong thematic focus for the course. Other instructors may feel comfortable setting aside three or four weeks toward the end of a semester to investigate a single issue, perhaps with a goal of a final project such as a longer oral or written assignment. Yet other instructors may structure their course around several of the books, perhaps making cross-references between related texts in different volumes of the series.

Format

Streamlines' major strengths include accessibility and ease of use, which stem in part from their consistent format. Each book is approximately 130 pages long, includes 14 to 18 readings, and contains a substantial, but not overwhelming apparatus—a brief introduction, five study and discussion questions, and two suggestions for writing projects for each reading selection. Several topics for thought, research, and writing at the end of each book help students synthesize the individual selections. The books introduce students to the subject matter of the volume with an initial poem. Every book is divided into four sections, which contain several thematically related works.

The Individual Readers

Learning This volume contains readings that address fundamental questions that philosophers, educators, and psychologists ask about how and why people learn, and examine events and attitudes that can make learning difficult as well as pleasurable. The issue of learning (both in and out of the classroom) is especially relevant for first-year composition students to examine in depth. The first section of the reader, "Learning from Experience," explores the learning that results from the revelations that arise from learning experiences. "Learning at School," the next section, focuses on classrooms and explores different aspects of them. "Learning and Diversity" considers ways that language, cultural, and class differences become issues in education, while the final section, "Thinking About How We Learn," looks at how intelligence is defined and how effective education programs can help to build strong communities.

Health   Students are concerned about many health issues, and we have tried to confront some of these concerns in this volume. The selections engage interest by closely viewing health concerns that are foremost in students' minds. The first section, "Doctors," examines how both caring, supportive relations with physicians and self-awareness figure into recovery processes. "Self Image and High-Risk Behavior" discusses relationships among self-esteem, body image, and wellness, while the third section, "Mental Health," examines relationships between psychological stress and physical illness as well as some of the symptoms, causes, and consequences of mental disorders such as depression and manic depression. The final section, "Healing and Community," provides a broader perspective on ways that doctors and patients can work together to create caring communities dedicated to good health.

Relationships   Relationship issues are particularly important to students trying to find their way in new campus communities. This volume begins with "Home and Family," exploring crucial relationships between parents and children as well as rituals and celebrations. "Friendships" examines adolescent and romantic relationships, while "Relationships at Work" examines work-related friendships as well as the self-understanding that may come through commitment to a meaningful vocation. The final section, "Community and Spirit," considers the complex network of relationships that exist between the individual and his or her communities of heritage, culture, and faith.

The Natural World   Nature inspires people of all ages; it is also an area for controversies and concerns about the use and preservation of species and ecosystems. This volume begins with an exploration of "The Experience of Nature," which includes inspirational narratives of travels in nature. The second section, "Nature and the Scientific Mind," explores the ways scientists perceive nature and theorize about natural processes. "Environmental Issues" presents students with controversies surrounding pollution, environmental disasters, and the movement to protect the earth and its species. Finally, in "Nature and the Philosophical Imagination," students are introduced to meditative essays that reflect on philosophical and spiritual meanings that can be found through contact with nature.

Work   Work issues are of special concern to students today—many of them are working part-time while attending college and anticipating the pressures of the job market after graduation. The first section, "Work and Youth," provides portraits of the job market and includes narratives about the kinds of summer job experiences with which students may be familiar. "Gender in the Workplace" focuses on sexual harassment and gender discrimination in work environments. The next section, "Job Preferences and Affirmative Action, presents experiences and arguments relative to issues of affirmative action in workplaces, while the readings in "The

Bottom Line" explore a variety of ethical concerns that affect both workers and managers.

Mass Culture and Electronic Media   At the heart of many students' cultural experiences are the electronic media—particularly radio, television, CDs, and the Internet. We begin this volume with "Cult Heroes and Icons," which presents readings that bridge discussions of the older heroes of the mass media of cartoons and comic books with heroes of the newer media. The second section, "Gender and Family Issues in the Electronic Media," provides analysis of the impact of the electronic media on women and family life. "Ethnicity and Electronic Media" reflects on media images of minority groups. Finally, in "Perceiving New Realities: Reading the New Electronic Media," media theorists and researchers discuss how television and the Internet influence our perceptions of reality and suggest ways to "read" the media insightfully in order to accurately discern underlying messages.

We would like to thank Alison Zetterquist, Jayne Fargnoli, Janet Edmonds, and Terri Teleen at Houghton Mifflin, our student writers, and Steven Lane, M.D. For helping us refine our ideas, we would also like to thank our reviewers:

James K. Bell, College of San Mateo

Donald Blount, University of South Carolina—Aiken

Keith Coplin, Colby Community College

Jan Delasara, Metropolitan State College of Denver

Patrick Dolan, Arapahoe Community College

Frank Fennell, Loyola University

Judith Funston, State University of New York at Potsdam

Sara McLaughlin, Texas Tech University

Denish Martone, New York University

Lawrence E. Musgrove, University of Southern Indiana

Julie Nichols, Okaloosa-Walton Community College

Pearlie M. Peters, Rider University

Katherine Ploeger, Modesto Junior College, California State University, Stanislaus

John Reilly, Loyola Marymount University

Patricia Roberts, Rivier College

Kristen Snoddy, Indiana University, Kokomo

Jan Strever, Gonzaga University

Any teacher can take a child to the classroom, but not every teacher can make him learn. He will not work joyously unless he feels that liberty is his. HELEN KELLER

Education as the practice of freedom becomes not a force which fragments or separates, but one that brings us closer, expanding our definitions of home and community. BELL HOOKS

For children, learning is natural, playful, and joyous. Children want to discover and understand the mysteries of their world. As we mature, learning becomes a challenge: Learning and knowing have been difficult for all of us at one time or another. The readings included in *Learning* address the fundamental questions that philosophers, educators, and psychologists have raised about how and why people learn and about what can block or prevent individuals from learning.

As you read this anthology, you will be joining an inquiry about the nature of learning that has been transforming humanity for centuries. First, however, consider your own educational goals and ideals: Why are you in school? Which of your classes and teachers have helped you to learn? Are you self-motivated to learn, or are you motivated by grades and the expectations of others? How do you think you will apply your college education after graduation? While each of us develops a special way of learning, extending our knowledge of the world and learning more about how we learn help us to mature and to develop a better understanding of the cultural, social, and political realities that shape the quality of life.

Learning from Experience

The opening section presents a range of awakenings, of revelatory learning experiences. In "The Most Important Day of My Life," Helen Keller describes how education brought about an inner awakening when her teacher Anne Sullivan showed her that love and learning are intimately connected, and Frederick Douglass, in a selection from his autobiography, "Learning to Read and Write," explains how he came to understand that learning to read would be his path out of slavery to freedom. In Maxine Hong Kingston's "The Silent Girl," the Asian American narrator expresses her own insecurity and self-hatred as she bullies another student who is much like herself. After this incident, the narrator must confront her own inner demons in order to come to a deeper self-understanding.

Learning at School

The readings in this section explore a range of perspectives on why and how students learn in classroom situations. The first two selections share the gifts that teachers can bring to their classrooms. In the first, "Corla Hawkins," social activist Jonathan Kozol captures the work of a gifted teacher. Working with children in an impoverished school district, Hawkins succeeds through her warmth, caring, and commitment to her students. Like Corla Hawkins, linguist Deborah Tannen, in "How Male and Female Students Use Language Differently," argues that small-group work and learning to respect and learn from one another are crucial to success in a coeducational classroom. In the section's final selection, "Possible Lives," Mike Rose explains why he finds hope in certain classrooms that "help us imagine—and, in imagining, struggle to achieve—what schools in the public domain . . . can be." Focusing his attention on the experiential aspects of learning, Rose asserts that a classroom should be a safe place where students' feelings and minds are respected, where they participate and help to solve problems.

Learning and Diversity

This section presents various educational situations and issues that encourage us to reflect on the complex problem of how an educational program can integrate the many different cultures that make up America. Maya Angelou, in "Graduation," shows how her high hopes and those of the black community were dismissed by the white politician speaking at her school graduation, but how she overcame her disillusionment and found strength in the wisdom and courage of her people. Richard Rodriguez, in "Private and Public Language," also writes about the problems that minority students face, in this case the problems they encounter when they attend a public school where they need to speak a language different from the one they speak at home. Rodriguez concludes that it is necessary for minority students to master the mainstream, public language, and that "not to understand this is to misunderstand the public uses of schooling and to trivialize the nature of intimate life." In "Keeping Close to Home: Class and Education," bell hooks acknowledges the class and race differences in public and private educational institutions.

Hooks believes that different social classes must enrich one another through mutual learning and understanding of differences. In "A Literary Debate," student writer David Champlin brings the voices of bell hooks and Frederick Douglass into a dialogue that suggests ways in which education can empower people and help them to respect cultures that are different from their own.

Thinking About How We Learn

This section explores issues related to how one learns, how intelligence is defined and assessed, and how educational situations can help to build stronger communities and revitalize moral energy. Howard Gardner, in "Multiple Intelligences," argues that determining intelligence is far more complex than giving an IQ test. Gardner delineates seven kinds of intelligence, promising that if we "can mobilize the spectrum of human abilities . . . people [will] feel better about themselves and more competent." Next, a leading proponent of a standardized core curriculum, E. D. Hirsch, Jr., in "The Common School and the Common Good," presents his position on the controversial issue of common national standards and course content. Critical of those teachers who terrify children, John Holt argues, in "On Discipline," that children learn best when they are self-motivated and find inner discipline.

Our intention in designing this collection of readings has been to help you to develop an understanding of how you learn and what type of education might be best for you. In a deeper sense, the readings are about love and hope, struggle and freedom, courage and belief in one's own values in the face of adversity, and about ways to help others find freedom and to build better communities.

When I Heard the Learn'd Astronomer

WALT WHITMAN

When I heard the learn'd astronomer,
When the proofs, the figures, were ranged in columns before me,
When I was shown the charts and diagrams, to add, divide, and
    measure them,
When I sitting heard the astronomer where he lectured with much   5
    applause in the lecture-room,
How soon unaccountable I became tired and sick,
Till rising and gliding out I wander'd off by myself,
In the mystical moist night-air, and from time to time,
Look'd up in perfect silence at the stars.   10

Learning from Experience

The Most Important Day of My Life

HELEN KELLER

Helen Keller is best known for her inspirational triumph over the limiting effects of deafness and blindness. Keller was born in 1880 in Tuscumbia, Alabama. She was a healthy child until the age of eighteen months, when scarlet fever left her deaf, blind, and mute. In The Story of My Life *(1902), Helen Keller wrote about her education, which began just before she was seven years old when she met Anne Mansfield Sullivan, who became her teacher and beloved friend. The two women maintained their relationship until Anne Sullivan's death in 1936. Helen Keller began her writing career, which was to last for more than fifty years, while she was a student at Radcliffe. During her lifetime many universities around the world awarded her honorary doctoral degrees. William Gibson's play and film,* The Miracle Worker, *have helped to make Anne Sullivan's successful awakening of Keller's mind into an inspirational story for millions. A eulogy at Helen Keller's funeral in 1968 captures the feelings of many people throughout the world: "Her spirit will endure as long as man can read and stories can be told of the woman who showed the world there are no boundaries to courage and faith."*

1   The most important day I remember in all my life is the one on which my teacher, Anne Mansfield Sullivan, came to me. I am filled with wonder when I consider the immeasurable contrasts between the two lives which it connects. It was the third of March, 1887, three months before I was seven years old.

2   On the afternoon of that eventful day, I stood on the porch, dumb, expectant. I guessed vaguely from my mother's signs and from the hurrying to and fro in the house that something unusual was about to happen, so I went to the door and waited on the steps. The afternoon sun penetrated the mass of honeysuckle that covered the porch, and fell on my upturned face. My fingers lingered almost unconsciously on the familiar leaves and blossoms which had just come forth to greet the sweet southern spring. I did not know what the future held of marvel or surprise for me. Anger and bitterness had preyed upon me continually for weeks and a deep languor had succeeded this passionate struggle.

3   Have you ever been at sea in a dense fog, when it seemed as if a tangible white darkness shut you in, and the great ship, tense and anxious, groped her way toward the shore with plummet and sounding-line, and you waited with beating heart for something to happen? I was like that ship before my education began, only I was without compass or sounding-line, and had no way of knowing how

near the harbour was. "Light! give me light!" was the wordless cry of my soul, and the light of love shone on me in that very hour.

I felt approaching footsteps. I stretched out my hand as I supposed to my mother. Some one took it, and I was caught up and held close in the arms of her who had come to reveal all things to me, and, more than all things else, to love me.

The morning after my teacher came she led me into her room and gave me a doll. The little blind children at the Perkins Institution had sent it and Laura Bridgman had dressed it; but I did not know this until afterward. When I had played with it a little while, Miss Sullivan slowly spelled into my hand the word "d-o-l-l." I was at once interested in this finger play and tried to imitate it. When I finally succeeded in making the letters correctly I was flushed with childish pleasure and pride. Running downstairs to my mother I held up my hand and made the letters for doll. I did not know that I was spelling a word or even that words existed; I was simply making my fingers go in monkey-like imitation. In the days that followed I learned to spell in this uncomprehending way a great many words, among them *pin*, *hat*, *cup* and a few verbs like *sit*, *stand* and *walk*. But my teacher had been with me several weeks before I understood that everything has a name.

One day, while I was playing with my new doll, Miss Sullivan put my big rag doll into my lap also, spelled, "d-o-l-l" and tried to make me understand that "d-o-l-l" applied to both. Earlier in the day we had had a tussle over the words "m-u-g" and "w-a-t-e-r." Miss Sullivan had tried to impress upon me that "m-u-g" is *mug* and that "w-a-t-e-r" is *water*, but I persisted in confounding the two. In despair she had dropped the subject for the time, only to renew it at the first opportunity. I became impatient at her repeated attempts and, seizing the new doll, I dashed it upon the floor. I was keenly delighted when I felt the fragments of the broken doll at my feet. Neither sorrow nor regret followed my passionate outburst. I had not loved the doll. In the still, dark world in which I lived there was no strong sentiment or tenderness. I felt my teacher sweep the fragments to one side of the hearth and I had a sense of satisfaction that the cause of my discomfort was removed. She brought me my hat, and I knew I was going out into the warm sunshine. This thought, if a wordless sensation may be called a thought, made me hop and skip with pleasure.

We walked down the path to the well-house, attracted by the fragrance of the honeysuckle with which it was covered. Someone was drawing water and my teacher placed my hand under the spout. As the cool stream gushed over one hand she spelled into the other the word *water*, first slowly, then rapidly. I stood still, my whole attention fixed upon the motions of her fingers. Suddenly I felt a misty consciousness as of something forgotten—a thrill of returning thought; and somehow the mystery of language was revealed to me. I knew then that "w-a-t-e-r" meant the wonderful cool something that was flowing over my hand. That living word awakened my soul, gave it light, hope, joy, set it free! There were barriers still, it is true, but barriers that could in time be swept away.

I left the well-house eager to learn. Everything had a name, and   8
each name gave birth to a new thought. As we returned to the house every object which I touched seemed to quiver with life. That was because I saw everything with the strange, new sight that had come to me. On entering the door I remembered the doll I had broken. I felt my way to the hearth and picked up the pieces. I tried vainly to put them together. Then my eyes filled with tears; for I realized what I had done; and for the first time I felt repentance and sorrow.

I learned a great many new words that day. I do not remember   9
what they all were; but I do know that *mother, father, sister, teacher* were among them—words that were to make the world blossom for me, "like Aaron's rod, with flowers." It would have been difficult to find a happier child than I was as I lay in my crib at the close of that eventful day and lived over the joys it had brought me, and for the first time longed for a new day to come. . . .

I recall many incidents of the summer of 1887 that followed my   10
soul's sudden awakening. I did nothing but explore with my hands and learn the name of every object that I touched; and the more I handled things and learned their names and uses, the more joyous and confident grew my sense of kinship with the rest of the world.

When the time of daisies and buttercups came Miss Sullivan took   11
me by the hand across the fields, where men were preparing the earth for the seed, to the banks of the Tennessee River, and there, sitting on the warm grass. I had my first lesson in the beneficence of nature. I learned how the sun and the rain make to grow out of the ground every tree that is pleasant to the sight and good for food, how birds build their nests and live and thrive from land to land, how the squirrel, the deer, the lion and every other creature finds food and shelter. As my knowledge of things grew I felt more and more the delight of the world I was in. Long before I learned to do a sum in arithmetic or describe the shape of the earth, Miss Sullivan had taught me to find beauty in the fragrant woods, in every blade of grass, and in the curves and dimples of my baby sister's hand. She linked my earliest thoughts with nature, and made me feel that "birds and flowers and I were happy peers."

But about this time I had an experience which taught me that nature   12
is not always kind. One day my teacher and I were returning from a long ramble. The morning had been fine, but it was growing warm and sultry when at last we turned our faces homeward. Two or three times we stopped to rest under a tree by the wayside. Our last halt was under a wild cherry tree a short distance from the house. The shade was grateful, and the tree was so easy to climb that with my teacher's assistance I was able to scramble to a seat in the branches. It was so cool up

in the tree that Miss Sullivan proposed that we have our luncheon there. I promised to keep still while she went to the house to fetch it.

Suddenly a change passed over the tree. All the sun's warmth left the air. I knew the sky was black, because all the heat, which meant light to me, had died out of the atmosphere. A strange odour came up from the earth. I knew it, it was the odour that always precedes a thunderstorm, and a nameless fear clutched at my heart. I felt absolutely alone, cut off from my friends and the firm earth. The immense, the unknown, enfolded me. I remained still and expectant; a chilling terror crept over me. I longed for my teacher's return; but above all things I wanted to get down from that tree. 13

There was a moment of sinister silence, then a multitudinous stirring of the leaves. A shiver ran through the tree, and the wind sent forth a blast that would have knocked me off had I not clung to the branch with might and main. The tree swayed and strained. The small twigs snapped and fell about me in showers. A wild impulse to jump seized me, but terror held me fast. I crouched down in the fork of the tree. The branches lashed about me. I felt the intermittent jarring that came now and then, as if something heavy had fallen and the shock traveled up till it reached the limb I sat on. It worked my suspense up to the highest point, and just as I was thinking the tree and I should fall together, my teacher seized my hand and helped me down. I clung to her, trembling with joy to feel the earth under my feet once more. I had learned a new lesson—that nature "wages open war against her children, and under softest touch hides treacherous claws." 14

After this experience it was a long time before I climbed another tree. The mere thought filled me with terror. It was the sweet allurement of the mimosa tree in full bloom that finally overcame my fears. One beautiful spring morning when I was alone in the summerhouse, reading, I became aware of a wonderful subtle fragrance in the air. I started up and instinctively stretched out my hands. It seemed as if the spirit of spring had passed through the summer-house. "What is it?" I asked, and the next minute I recognized the odour of the mimosa blossoms. I felt my way to the end of the garden, knowing that the mimosa tree was near the fence, at the turn of the path. Yes, there it was, all quivering in the warm sunshine, its blossom-laden branches almost touching the long grass. Was there ever anything so exquisitely beautiful in the world before! Its delicate blossoms shrank from the slightest earthly touch; it seemed as if a tree of paradise had been transplanted to earth. I made my way through a shower of petals to the great trunk and for one minute stood irresolute; then, putting my foot in the broad space between the forked branches, I pulled myself up into the tree. I had some difficulty in holding on, for the branches were very large and the bark hurt my hands. But I had a delicious sense that I was doing something unusual and wonderful, so I kept on climbing higher and higher, until 15

I reached a little seat which somebody had built there so long ago that it had grown part of the tree itself. I sat there for a long, long time, feeling like a fairy on a rosy cloud. After that I spent many happy hours in my tree of paradise, thinking fair thoughts and dreaming bright dreams. . . .

I had now the key to all language, and I was eager to learn to use it.   16
Children who hear acquire language without any particular effort; the words that fall from others' lips they catch on the wing, as it were, delightedly, while the little deaf child must trap them by a slow and often painful process. But whatever the process, the result is wonderful. Gradually from naming an object we advance step by step until we have traversed the vast distance between our first stammered syllable and the sweep of thought in a line of Shakespeare.

At first, when my teacher told me about a new thing I asked very   17
few questions. My ideas were vague, and my vocabulary was inadequate; but as my knowledge of things grew, and I learned more and more words, my field of inquiry broadened, and I would return again and again to the same subject, eager for further information. Sometimes a new word revived an image that some earlier experience had engraved on my brain.

I remember the morning that I first asked the meaning of the word,   18
"love." This was before I knew many words. I had found a few early violets in the garden and brought them to my teacher. She tried to kiss me; but at that time I did not like to have any one kiss me except my mother. Miss Sullivan put her arm gently round me and spelled into my hand, "I love Helen."

"What is love?" I asked.   19

She drew me closer to her and said, "It is here," pointing to my   20
heart, whose beats I was conscious of for the first time. Her words puzzled me very much because I did not then understand anything unless I touched it.

I smelt the violets in her hand and asked, half in words, half in   21
signs, a question which meant, "Is love the sweetness of flowers?"

"No," said my teacher.   22

Again I thought. The warm sun was shining on us.   23

"Is this not love?" I asked, pointing in the direction from which the   24
heat came, "Is this not love?"

It seemed to me that there could be nothing more beautiful than   25
the sun, whose warmth makes all things grow. But Miss Sullivan shook her head, and I was greatly puzzled and disappointed. I thought it strange that my teacher could not show me love.

A day or two afterward I was stringing beads of different sizes in   26
symmetrical groups—two large beads, three small ones, and so on. I had made many mistakes, and Miss Sullivan had pointed them out again and again with gentle patience. Finally I noticed a very obvious error in the sequence and for an instant I concentrated my attention

on the lesson and tried to think how I should have arranged the beads. Miss Sullivan touched my forehead and spelled with decided emphasis, "Think."

In a flash I knew that the word was the name of the process that was going on in my head. This was my first conscious perception of an abstract idea.   27

For a long time I was still—I was not thinking of the beads in my lap, but trying to find a meaning for "love" in light of this new idea. The sun had been under a cloud all day, and there had been brief showers; but suddenly the sun broke forth in all its southern splendour.   28

Again I asked my teacher, "Is this not love?"   29

"Love is something like the clouds that were in the sky before the sun came out," she replied. Then in simpler words than these, which at that time I could not have understood, she explained: "You cannot touch the clouds, you know; but you feel the rain and know how glad the flowers and the thirsty earth are to have it after a hot day. You cannot touch love either; but you feel the sweetness that it pours into everything. Without love you would not be happy or want to play."   30

The beautiful truth burst upon my mind—I felt that there were invisible lines that stretched between my spirit and the spirits of others.   31

From the beginning of my education Miss Sullivan made it a practice to speak to me as she would speak to any hearing child; the only difference was that she spelled the sentences into my hand instead of speaking them. If I did not know the words and idioms necessary to express my thoughts she supplied them, even suggesting conversation when I was unable to keep up my end of the dialogue.   32

This process was continued for several years; for the deaf child does not learn in a month, or even in two or three years, the numberless idioms and expressions used in the simplest daily intercourse. The little hearing child learns these from constant repetition and imitation. The conversation he hears in his home stimulates his mind and suggests topics and calls forth the spontaneous expression of his own thoughts. This natural exchange of ideas is denied to the deaf child. My teacher, realizing this, determined to supply the kinds of stimuli I lacked. This she did by repeating to me as far as possible, verbatim, what she heard, and by showing me how I could take part in the conversation. But it was a long time before I ventured to take the initiative, and still longer before I could find something appropriate to say at the right time.   33

The deaf and the blind find it very difficult to acquire the amenities of conversation. How much more this difficulty must be augmented in the case of those who are both deaf and blind! They cannot distinguish the tone of the voice or, without assistance, go up and down the gamut of tones that give significance to words; nor can they watch the expression of the speaker's face, and a look is often the very soul of what one says. . . .   34

Thus I learned from life itself. At the beginning I was only a little   35
mass of possibilities. It was my teacher who unfolded and developed
them. When she came, everything about me breathed of love and joy
and was full of meaning. She has never since let pass an opportunity
to point out the beauty that is in everything, nor has she ceased trying
in thought and action and example to make my life sweet and useful.

It was my teacher's genius, her quick sympathy, her loving tact   36
which made the first years of my education so beautiful. It was because she seized the right moment to impart knowledge that made it
so pleasant and acceptable to me. She realized that a child's mind is
like a shallow brook which ripples and dances merrily over the stony
course of its education and reflects hear a flower, there a bush, yonder
a fleecy cloud; and she attempted to guide my mind on its way, knowing that like a brook it should be fed by mountain streams and hidden
springs, until it broadened out into a deep river, capable of reflecting
on its placid surface, billowy hills, the luminous shadows of trees and
the blue heavens, as well as the sweet face of a little flower.

Any teacher can take a child to the classroom, but not every teacher   37
can make him learn. He will not work joyously unless he feels that
liberty is his, whether he is busy or at rest; he must feel the flush of
victory and the heart-sinking of disappointment before he takes with
a will the tasks distasteful to him and resolves to dance his way
bravely through a dull routine of textbooks.

My teacher is so near to me that I scarcely think of myself apart   38
from her. How much of my delight in all beautiful things is innate, and
how much is due to her influence, I can never tell. I feel that her being
is inseparable from my own, and that the footsteps of my life are in
hers. All the best of me belongs to her—there is not a talent, or an in-
spiration or a joy in me that has not awakened by her loving touch.

QUESTIONS FOR DISCUSSION

1   Why have words become for Keller "the key to all knowledge"? How
    has her understanding of the role of words awakened her soul?

2   What qualities and techniques make Miss Sullivan a successful
    teacher? What is the most important lesson that Miss Sullivan
    teaches Helen? Compare and contrast Miss Sullivan with one of
    your favorite teachers.

3   What role does frustration play in Helen Keller's learning process?
    How does she overcome her setbacks? Refer to specific examples
    in the selection to support your point of view.

4   Could Miss Sullivan's approach to teaching be used in a public
    school classroom? Explain your position.

5   Why is comprehending language and conversation especially
    challenging for blind and deaf people? In what ways does reading

about Helen Keller's struggle help you to understand and appreciate the importance of language? Frame your answer in a specific situation or situations.

| IDEAS FOR WRITING |

1   Write an essay about a person who has helped you to learn, to develop your mind and spirit.
2   Write an essay in which you analyze Miss Sullivan's teaching style. Then discuss how her approach could be applied to enliven classes at a school you have attended or are attending.

Learning To Read and Write

FREDERICK DOUGLASS

An important figure in the history of African American thought and writing, Frederick Douglass (1818–1895) was born into slavery in Maryland. After escaping to the North, he wrote of his journey to freedom in The Narrative Life of Frederick Douglass *(1845). As the publisher of the newspapers* North Star *and* Frederick Douglass' Paper, *Douglass had an important impact on the antislavery movement. He also worked as a major stationmaster on the Underground Railroad, helping hundreds of slaves make their way to freedom. During the Civil War he served as an adviser to President Abraham Lincoln. After 1872, Douglass worked as an international diplomat. In the following selection from his autobiography, you will learn about how Douglass's struggle to educate himself in the face of unrelenting prejudice helped to develop his character and his mind.*

I lived in Master Hugh's family about seven years. During this time, I succeeded in learning to read and write. In accomplishing this, I was compelled to resort to various stratagems. I had no regular teacher. My mistress, who kindly commenced to instruct me, had, in compliance with the advice and direction of her husband, not only ceased to instruct, but had set her face against my being instructed by any one else. It is due, however, to my mistress to say of her, that she did not adopt this course of treatment immediately. She at first lacked the depravity indispensable to shutting me up in mental darkness. It was at least necessary for her to have some training in the exercise of irresponsible power, to make her equal to the task of treating me as though I were a brute.

My mistress was, as I have said, a kind and tender-hearted woman; and in the simplicity of her soul she commenced, when I first went to live with her, to treat me as she supposed one human being ought to treat another. In entering upon the duties of a slaveholder, she did not seem to perceive that I sustained to her the relation of a mere chattel, and that for her to treat me as a human being was not only wrong, but dangerously so. Slavery proved as injurious to her as it did to me. When I went there, she was a pious, warm, and tender-hearted woman. There was no sorrow or suffering for which she had not a tear. She had bread for the hungry, clothes for the naked, and comfort for every mourner that came within her reach. Slavery soon proved its ability to divest her of these heavenly qualities. Under its influence, the tender heart became stone, and the lamb-like disposition gave way to one of tiger-like fierceness. The first step in her downward course was in her ceasing to instruct me. She now commenced to practise her husband's precepts. She finally became even more violent in her opposition than her husband himself. She was not satisfied with simply doing as well as he had commanded; she seemed anxious to do better. Nothing seemed to make her more angry than to see me with a newspaper. She seemed to think that here lay the danger. I have had her rush at me with a face made all up of fury, and snatch from me a newspaper, in a manner that fully revealed her apprehension. She was an apt woman; and a little experience soon demonstrated, to her satisfaction, that education and slavery were incompatible with each other.

From this time I was most narrowly watched. If I was in a separate room any considerable length of time, I was sure to be suspected of having a book, and was at once called to give an account of myself. All this, however, was too late. The first step had been taken. Mistress, in teaching me the alphabet, had given me the *inch*, and no precaution could prevent me from taking the *ell*.

The plan which I adopted, and the one by which I was most successful, was that of making friends of all the little white boys whom I met in the street. As many of these as I could, I converted into teachers. With their kindly aid, obtained at different times and in different places, I finally succeeded in learning to read. When I was sent on errands, I always took my book with me, and by doing one part of my errand quickly, I found time to get a lesson before my return. I used also to carry bread with me, enough of which was always in the house, and to which I was always welcome; for I was much better off in this regard than many of the poor white children in our neighborhood. This bread I used to bestow upon the hungry little urchins, who, in return, would give me that more valuable bread of knowledge. I am strongly tempted to give the names of two or three of those little boys, as a testimonial of the gratitude and affection I bear them; but prudence forbids;—not that it would injure me, but it might embarrass them; for it is almost an unpardonable offence to teach slaves to read in this Christian country. It is enough to say of the dear little fellows, that they lived on Philpot Street, very near Durgin and Bailey's shipyard. I used to talk this matter of slavery over with them. I would sometimes say to them, I wished I could be as free as they would be when they got to be men. "You will be free as soon as you are twenty-one, *but I am a slave for life!* Have not I as good a right to be free as you have?" These words used to trouble them; they would express for me the liveliest sympathy, and console me with the hope that something would occur by which I might be free.

I was now about twelve years old, and the thought of being *a slave for life* began to bear heavily upon my heart. Just about this time, I got hold of a book entitled "The Columbian Orator." Every opportunity I got, I used to read this book. Among much of other interesting matter, I found in it a dialogue between a master and his slave. The slave was represented as having run away from his master three times. The dialogue represented the conversation which took place between them, when the slave was retaken the third time. In this dialogue, the whole argument in behalf of slavery was brought forward by the master, all of which was disposed of by the slave. The slave was made to say some very smart as well as impressive things in reply to his master—things which had the desired though unexpected effect; for the conversation resulted in the voluntary emancipation of the slave on the part of the master.

In the same book, I met with one of Sheridan's mighty speeches on   6 and in behalf of Catholic emancipation. These were choice documents to me. I read them over and over again with unabated interest. They gave tongue to interesting thoughts of my own soul, which had frequently flashed through my mind, and died away for want of utterance. The moral which I gained from the dialogue was the power of truth over the conscience of even a slaveholder. What I got from Sheridan was a bold denunciation of slavery, and a powerful vindication of human rights. The reading of these documents enabled me to utter my thoughts, and to meet the arguments brought forward to sustain slavery; but while they relieved me of one difficulty, they brought another even more painful than the one of which I was relieved. The more I read, the more I was led to abhor and detest my enslavers. I could regard them in no other light than a band of successful robbers, who had left their homes, and gone to Africa, and stolen us from our homes, and in a strange land reduced us to slavery. I loathed them as being the meanest as well as the most wicked of men. As I read and contemplated the subject, behold! that very discontentment which Master Hugh had predicted would follow my learning to read had already come, to torment and sting my soul to unutterable anguish. As I writhed under it, I would at times feel that learning to read had been a curse rather than a blessing. It had given me a view of my wretched condition, without the remedy. It opened my eyes to the horrible pit, but to no ladder upon which to get out. In moments of agony, I envied my fellow-slaves for their stupidity. I have often wished myself a beast. I preferred the condition of the meanest reptile to my own. Any thing, no matter what, to get rid of thinking! It was this everlasting thinking of my condition that tormented me. There was no getting rid of it. It was pressed upon me by every object within sight or hearing, animate or inanimate. The silver trump of freedom had roused my soul to eternal wakefulness. Freedom now appeared, to disappear no more forever. It was heard in every sound, and seen in every thing. It was ever present to torment me with a sense of my wretched condition. I saw nothing without seeing it, I heard nothing without hearing it, and felt nothing without feeling it. It looked from every star, it smiled in every calm, breathed in every wind, and moved in every storm.

I often found myself regretting my own existence, and wishing my-   7
self dead; and but for the hope of being free, I have no doubt but that
I should have killed myself, or done something for which I should
have been killed. While in this state of mind, I was eager to hear anyone speak of slavery. I was a ready listener. Every little while, I could
hear something about the abolitionists. It was some time before I
found what the word meant. It was always used in such connections
to make it an interesting word to me. If a slave ran away and succeeded in getting clear, or if a slave killed his master, set fire to a barn,
or did anything wrong in the mind of a slaveholder, it was spoken of as
the fruit of *abolition*. Hearing the word in this connection very often, I
set about learning what it meant. The dictionary afforded me little or
no help. I found it was "the act of abolishing;" but then I did not know
what was to be abolished. Here I was perplexed. I did not dare to ask
any one about its meaning, for I was satisfied that it was something
they wanted me to know very little about. After a patient waiting, I got
one of our city papers, containing an account of the number of peti-
tions from the north, praying for the abolition of slavery in the District
of Columbia, and of the slave trade between the States. From this time
I understood the words *abolition* and *abolitionist*, and always drew
near when that word was spoken, expecting to hear something of importance to myself and fellow-slaves. The light broke in upon me by
degrees. I went one day down on the wharf of Mr. Waters; and seeing
two Irishmen unloading a scow of stone, I went, unasked, and helped
them. When we had finished, one of them came to me and asked me if
I were a slave. I told him I was. He asked, "Are ye a slave for life?" I told
him that I was. The good Irishman seemed to be deeply affected by the
statement. He said to the other that it was a pity so fine a fellow as myself should be a slave for life. He said it was a shame to hold me. They
both advised me to run away to the north; that I should find friends
there, and that I should be free. I pretended not to be interested in
what they said, and treated them as if I did not understand them; for I
feared they might be treacherous. White men have been known to encourage slaves to escape, and then, to get the reward, catch them and
return them to their masters. I was afraid that these seemingly good
men might use me so; but I nevertheless remembered their advice,
and from that time I resolved to run away. I looked forward to a time at
which it would be safe for me to escape. I was too young to think of
doing so immediately; besides, I wished to learn how to write, as I
might have occasion to write my own pass. I consoled myself with the
hope that I should one day find a good chance. Meanwhile, I would
learn to write.

The idea as to how I might learn to write was suggested to me by   8
being in Durgin and Bailey's ship-yard, and frequently seeing the ship
carpenters, after hewing, and getting a piece of timber ready for use,

write on the timber the name of that part of the ship for which it was intended. When a piece of timber was intended for the larboard side, it would be marked thus—"L." When a piece was for the starboard side, it would be marked thus—"S." A piece for the larboard side forward, would be marked thus—"L. F." When a piece was for starboard side forward, it would be marked thus—"S. F." For larboard aft, it would be marked thus—"L. A." For starboard aft, it would be marked thus—"S. A." I soon learned the names of these letters, and for what they were intended when placed upon a piece of timber in the ship-yard. I immediately commenced copying them, and in a short time was able to make the four letters named. After that, when I met with any boy who I knew could write, I would tell him I could write as well as he. The next word would be, "I don't believe you. Let me see you try it." I would then make the letters which I had been so fortunate as to learn, and ask him to beat that. In this way I got a good many lessons in writing, which it is quite possible I should never have gotten in any other way. During this time, my copy-book was the board fence, brick wall, and pavement; my pen and ink was a lump of chalk. With these, I learned mainly how to write. I then commenced and continued copying the Italics in Webster's Spelling Book, until I could make them all without looking on the book. By this time, my little Master Thomas had gone to school, and learned how to write, and had written over a number of copy-books. These had been brought home, and shown to some of our near neighbors, and then laid aside. My mistress used to go to class meeting at the Wilk Street meeting-house every Monday afternoon, and leave me to take care of the house. When left thus, I used to spend the time in writing in the spaces left in Master Thomas's copy-book, copying what he had written. I continued to do this until I could write a hand very similar to that of Master Thomas. Thus, after a long, tedious effort for years, I finally succeeded in learning how to write.

QUESTIONS FOR DISCUSSION

1 Why does the relationship between Frederick Douglass and his mistress change? What is the nature of their power struggle?

2 Discuss several of the episodes that reflect Douglass's resourcefulness and his ability to learn from his experiences. Which incidents show that Douglass is a good listener and a good critical thinker?

3 Why is Douglass tormented by what he has learned through reading and thinking? How does he combat the frustrations that he must face on his journey to becoming an educated man?

4 Why and how does Douglass learn to write? What does his success suggest about his character?

5   What connections between freedom and education does Douglass make in this excerpt? What relationships between freedom and education do you see in your own life?

IDEAS FOR WRITING

1   Becoming educated helped Douglass to gain his freedom. What have you learned from his struggle? Write an essay that explores different ways in which your education, and reading and writing in particular, has helped you to gain more freedom and independence.

2   Using the resources of your local library and/or the Internet, find out more about how slaves learned to read and write, and how their education helped them to gain their freedom. Write an essay that presents your evidence and draws conclusions.

The Silent Girl

MAXINE HONG KINGSTON

Maxine Hong Kingston achieved acclaim with her first book,
Woman Warrior: Memoirs of a Girlhood Among Ghosts *(1976),*
which won the National Book Critics Circle award and was named
one of the top ten nonfiction works of the 1970s. Born in Stockton,
California, in 1940, Maxine Hong Kingston was the first of six
American-born children in her family; her parents were Chinese
immigrants, and Hong Kingston's first language was Cantonese.
After graduating from the University of California at Berkeley (1962)
with a degree in English literature, she went on to earn teaching
credentials and then moved to Hawaii, where she taught high school
for ten years. Woman Warrior *was published while Hong Kingston*
was teaching creative writing at a private university in California.
Her success as a writer has allowed her to write full time. Her subse-
quent works include China Men *(1980),* Hawaii One Summer *(1987),*
and Tripmaster Monkey: His Fake Book *(1988). The following selec-*
tion from Woman Warrior *will introduce you to her intensely detailed,*
emotional, and complex style, as well as to universal anxieties of
young adolescents.

She was a year older than I and was in my class for twelve years.   1
During all those years she read aloud but would not talk. Her older
sister was usually beside her; their parents kept the older daughter
back to protect the younger one. They were six and seven years old
when they began school. Although I had flunked kindergarten, I was
the same age as most other students in our class; my parents probably
lied about my age, so I had had a head start and came out even. My
younger sister was in the class below me; we were normal ages and
normally separated. The parents of the quiet girl, on the other hand,
protected both daughters. When it sprinkled, they kept them home
from school. The girls did not work for a living the way we did. But in
other ways we were the same.

We were similar in sports. We held the bat on our shoulders until we   2
walked to first base. (You got a strike only when you actually struck at
the ball.) Sometimes the pitcher wouldn't bother to throw to us. "Automatic walk," the other children would call, sending us on our way. By
fourth or fifth grade, though, some of us would try to hit the ball. "Easy
out," the other kids would say. I hit the ball a couple of times. Baseball
was nice in that there was a definite spot to run to after hitting the
ball. Basketball confused me because when I caught the ball I didn't
know whom to throw it to. "Me. Me," the kids would be yelling. "Over
here." Suddenly it would occur to me I hadn't memorized which

ghosts were on my team and which were on the other. When the kids said, "Automatic walk," the girl who was quieter than I kneeled with one end of the bat in each hand and placed it carefully on the plate. Then she dusted her hands as she walked to first base, where she rubbed her hands softly, fingers spread. She always got tagged out before second base. She would whisper-read but not talk. Her whisper was as soft as if she had no muscles. She seemed to be breathing from a distance. I heard no anger or tension.

I joined in at lunchtime when the other students, the Chinese too, talked about whether or not she was mute, although obviously she was not if she could read aloud. People told how *they* had tried *their* best to be friendly. *They* said hello, but if she refused to answer, well, they didn't see why they had to say hello anymore. She had no friends of her own but followed her sister everywhere, although people and she herself probably thought I was her friend. I also followed her sister about, who was fairly normal. She was almost two years older and read more than anyone else.

I hated the younger sister, the quiet one. I hated her when she was the last chosen for her team and I, the last chosen for my team. I hated her for her China doll hair cut. I hated her at music time for the wheezes that came out of her plastic flute.

One afternoon in the sixth grade (that year I was arrogant with talk, not knowing there were going to be high school dances and college seminars to set me back), I and my little sister and the quiet girl and her big sister stayed late after school for some reason. The cement was cooling, and the tetherball poles made shadows across the gravel. The hooks at the rope ends were clinking against the poles. We shouldn't have been so late; there was laundry work to do and Chinese school to get to by 5:00. The last time we had stayed late, my mother had phoned the police and told them we had been kidnapped by bandits. The radio stations broadcast our descriptions. I had to get home before she did that again. But sometimes if you loitered long enough in the schoolyard, the other children would have gone home and you could play with the equipment before the office took it away. We were chasing one another through the playground and in and out of the basement, where the playroom and lavatory were. During the air raid drills (it was during the Korean War, which you knew about because every day the front page of the newspaper printed a map of Korea with the top part red and going up and down like a window shade), we curled up in this basement. Now everyone was gone. The playroom was army green and had nothing in it but a long trough with drinking spigots in rows. Pipes across the ceiling led to the drinking fountains and to the toilets in the next room. When someone flushed you could hear the water and other matter, which the children named, running inside the big pipe above the drinking spigots. There was one playroom for girls next to the girls' lavatory and one playroom for boys next to the boys' lavatory. The stalls were open and the toilets had no lids, by which we knew that ghosts have no sense of shame or privacy.

Inside the playroom the lightbulbs in cages had already been 6
turned off. Daylight came in x-patterns through the caging at the windows. I looked out and, seeing no one in the schoolyard, ran outside to climb the fire escape upside down, hanging on to the metal stairs with fingers and toes.

I did a flip off the fire escape and ran across the schoolyard. The day 7
was a great eye, and it was not paying much attention to me now. I could disappear with the sun; I could turn quickly sideways and slip into a different world. It seemed I could run faster this time, and by evening I would be able to fly. As the afternoon wore on we could run into the forbidden places—the boys' big yard, the boys' playroom. We could go into the boys' lavatory and look at the urinals. The only time during school hours I had crossed the boys' yard was when a flatbed truck with a giant thing covered with canvas and tied down with ropes had parked across the street. The children had told one another that it was a gorilla in captivity; we couldn't decide whether the sign said "Trail of the Gorilla" or "Trial of the Gorilla." The thing was as big as a house. The teachers couldn't stop us from hysterically rushing to the fence and clinging to the wire mesh. Now I ran across the boys' yard clear to the Cyclone fence and thought about the hair that I had seen sticking out of the canvas. It was going to be summer soon, so you could feel that freedom coming on too.

I ran back into the girls' yard, and there was the quiet sister all by 8
herself. I ran past her, and she followed me into the girls' lavatory. My footsteps rang hard against cement and tile because of the taps I had nailed into my shoes. Her footsteps were soft, padding after me. There was no one in the lavatory but the two of us. I ran all around the rows of twenty-five open stalls to make sure of that. No sisters. I think we must have been playing hide-and-go-seek. She was not good at hiding by herself and usually followed her sister; they'd hide in the same place. They must have gotten separated. In this growing twilight, a child could hide and never be found.

I stopped abruptly in front of the sinks, and she came running 9
toward me before she could stop herself, so that she almost collided with me. I walked closer. She backed away, puzzlement, then alarm in her eyes.

"You're going to talk," I said, my voice steady and normal, as it is when 10
talking to the familiar, the weak, and the small. "I am going to make you talk, you sissy-girl." She stopped backing away and stood fixed.

I looked into her face so I could hate it up close. She wore black 11
bangs, and her cheeks were pink and white. She was baby-soft. I thought that I could put my thumb on her nose and push it bonelessly in, indent her face. I could poke dimples into her cheeks. I could work her face around like dough. She stood still, and I did not want to look at

her face anymore; I hated fragility. I walked around her, looked her up and down the way the Mexican and Negro girls did when they fought, so tough. I hated her weak neck, the way it did not support her head but let it droop; her head would fall backward. I stared at the curve of her nape. I wished I was able to see what my own neck looked like from the back and sides. I hoped it did not look like hers; I wanted a stout neck. I grew my hair long to hide it in case it was a flower-stem neck. I walked around to the front of her to hate her face some more.

I reached up and took the fatty part of her cheek, not dough, but   12
meat, between my thumb and finger. This close, and I saw no pores. "Talk," I said. "Are you going to talk?" Her skin was fleshy, like squid out of which the glassy blades of bones had been pulled. I wanted tough skin, hard brown skin. I had callused my hands; I scratched dirt to blacken the nails, which I cut straight across to make stubby fingers. I gave her face a squeeze. "Talk." When I let go, the pink rushed back into my white thumbprint on her skin. I walked around to her side. "Talk!" I shouted into the side of her head. Her straight hair hung, the same all these years, no ringlets or braids or permanents. I squeezed the other cheek. "Are you? Huh? Are you going to talk?" She tried to shake her head, but I had hold of her face. She had no muscles to jerk away. Her skin seemed to stretch. I let her go in horror. What if it came away in my hand? "No, huh?" I said, rubbing the touch of her off my fingers. "Say 'No,' then," I said. I gave her another pinch and a twist. "Say 'No.'" She shook her head, her straight hair turning with her head, not swinging side to side like the pretty girls'. She was so neat. Her neatness bothered me. I hated the way she folded the wax paper from her lunch; she did not wad her brown paper bag and her school papers. I hated her clothes—the blue pastel cardigan, the white blouse with the collar that lay flat over the cardigan, the homemade flat, cotton skirt she wore when everybody else was wearing flared skirts. I hated pastels; I would wear black always. I squeezed again, harder, even though her cheek had a weak rubbery feeling I did not like. I squeezed one cheek, then the other, back and forth until the tears ran out of her eyes as if I had pulled them out. "Stop crying," I said, but although she habitually followed me around, she did not obey. Her eyes dripped; her nose dripped. She wiped her eyes with her papery fingers. The skin on her hands and arms seemed powdery-dry, like tracing paper, onion paper. I hated her fingers. I could snap them like breadsticks. I pushed her hands down. "Say 'Hi,'" I said. "'Hi.' Like that. Say your name. Go ahead. Say it. Or are you stupid? You're so stupid, you don't know your own name, is that it? When I say, 'What's your name?' you just blurt it out, O.K.? What's your name?" Last year the whole class had laughed at a boy who couldn't fill out a form because he didn't know his father's name. The teacher sighed, exasperated and was very sarcastic, "Don't you notice things? What does your mother call him?" she said. The

class laughed at how dumb he was not to notice things. "She calls him father of me," he said. Even we laughed although we knew that his mother did not call his father by name, and a son does not know his father's name. We laughed and were relieved that our parents had the foresight to tell us some names we could give the teachers. "If you're not stupid," I said to the quiet girl, "what's your name?" She shook her head, and some hair caught in her tears; wet black hair stuck to the side of the pink and white face. I reached up (she was taller than I) and took a strand of hair. I pulled it. "Well, then, let's honk your hair," I said. "Honk. Honk." Then I pulled the other side—"ho-o-n-nk"—a long pull; "ho-o-n-n-nk"—a longer pull. I could see her little white ears, like white cutworms curled under-neath the hair. "Talk!" I yelled into each cutworm.

I looked right at her. "I know you talk," I said. "I've heard you." Her   13
eyebrows flew up. Something in those black eyes was startled, and I pursued it. "I was walking past you house when you didn't know I was there. I heard you yell in English and in Chinese. You weren't just talk-ing. You were shouting. I heard you shout. You were saying, 'Where are you?' Say that again. Go ahead, just the way you did at home." I yanked harder on the hair, but steadily, not jerking. I did not want to pull it out. "Go ahead. Say, 'Where are you?' Say it loud enough for your sister to come. Call her. Make her come help you. Call her name. I'll stop if she comes. So call. Go ahead."

She shook her head, her mouth curved down, crying. I could see   14
her tiny white teeth, baby teeth. I wanted to grow big strong yellow teeth. "You do have a tongue," I said. "So use it." I pulled the hair at her temples, pulled the tears out of her eyes. "Say, 'Ow'" I said. "Just 'Ow.' Say, 'Let go.' Go ahead. Say it. I'll honk you again if you don't say, 'Let me alone.' Say, 'Leave me alone,' and I'll let you go. I will. I'll let go if you say it. You can stop this anytime you want to, you know. All you have to do is tell me to stop. Just say, 'Stop.' You're just asking for it, aren't you? You're just asking for another honk. Well, then, I'll have to give you another honk. Say, 'Stop.'" But she didn't. I had to pull again and again.

Sounds did come out of her mouth, sobs, chokes, noises that were   15
almost words. Snot ran out of her nose. She tried to wipe it on her hands, but there was too much of it. She used her sleeve. "You're dis-gusting," I told her. "Look at you, snot streaming down you nose, and you won't say a word to stop it. You're such a nothing." I moved behind her and pulled the hair growing out of her weak neck. I let go. I stood silent for a long time. Then I screamed, "Talk!" I would scare the words out of her. If she had had little bound feet, the toes twisted under the balls, I would have jumped up and landed on them—crunch!—stomped on them with my iron shoes. She cried hard, sobbing aloud. "Cry, 'Mama,'" I said. "Come on. Cry, 'Mama.' Say, 'Stop it.'"

I put my finger on her pointed chin. "I don't like you. I don't like   16
the weak little toots you make on your flute. Wheeze. Wheeze. I don't
like the way you don't swing at the ball. I don't like the way you're the
last one chosen. I don't like the way you can't make a fist for tetherball.
Why don't you make a fist? Come on. Get tough. Come on. Throw
fists." I pushed at her long hands; they swung limply at her sides. Her
fingers were so long, I thought maybe they had an extra joint. They
couldn't possibly make fists like other people's. "Make a fist," I said.
"Come on. Just fold those fingers up; fingers on the inside, thumbs on
the outside. Say something. Honk me back. You're so tall, and you let
me pick on you.

"Would you like a hanky? I can't get you one with embroidery on it   17
or crocheting along the edges, but I'll get you some toilet paper if you
tell me to. Go ahead. Ask me. I'll get it for you if you ask." She did not
stop crying. "Why don't you scream, 'Help'?" I suggested. "Say, 'Help.'
Go ahead." She cried on. "O.K. O.K. Don't talk. Just scream, and I'll let
you go. Won't that feel good? Go ahead. Like this." I screamed not too
loudly. My voice hit the tile and rang it as if I had thrown a rock at it.
The stalls opened wider and the toilets wider and darker. Shadows
leaned at angles I had not seen before. I was very late. Maybe a janitor
had locked me in with this girl for the night. Her black eyes blinked
and stared, blinked and stared. I felt dizzy from hunger. We had been
in this lavatory together forever. My mother would call the police
again if I didn't bring my sister home soon. "I'll let you go if you say
just one word," I said. "You can even say 'a' or 'the,' and I'll let you go.
Come on. Please." She didn't shake her head anymore, only cried
steadily, so much water coming out of her. I could see the two duct
holes where the tears welled out. Quarts of tears but no words. I
grabbed her by the shoulder. I could feel bones. The light was coming
in queerly through the frosted glass with the chicken wire embedded
in it. Her crying was like an animal's—a seal's—and it echoed around
the basement. "Do you want to stay here all night?" I asked. "Your
mother is wondering what happened to her baby. You wouldn't want
to have her mad at you. You'd better say something." I shook her
shoulder. I pulled her hair again. I squeezed her face. "Come on! Talk!
Talk! Talk!" She didn't seem to feel it anymore when I pulled her hair.
"There's nobody here but you and me. This isn't a classroom or a playground or a crowd. I'm just one person. You can talk in front of one
person. Don't make me pull harder and harder until you talk." But her
hair seemed to stretch; she did not say a word. "I'm going to pull
harder. Don't make me pull anymore, or your hair will come out and
you're going to be bald. Do you want to be bald? You don't want to be
bald, do you?"

Far away, coming from the edge of town, I heard whistles blow. The   18
cannery was changing shifts, letting out the afternoon people, and

still we were here at school. It was a sad sound—work done. The air was lonelier after the sound died.

"Why won't you talk?" I started to cry. What if I couldn't stop, and everyone would want to know what happened? "Now look what you've done," I scolded. "You're going to pay for this. I want to know why. And you're going to tell me why. You don't see I'm trying to help you out, do you? Do you want to be like this, dumb (do you know what dumb means?), your whole life? Don't you ever want to be a cheerleader? Or a pompom girl? What are you going to do for a living? Yeah, you're going to have to work because you can't be a housewife. Somebody has to marry you before you can be a housewife. And you, you are a plant. Do you know that? That's all you are if you don't talk. If you don't talk, you can't have a personality. You'll have no personality and no hair. You've got to let people know you have a personality and a brain. You think somebody is going to take care of you all your stupid life? You think you'll always have your big sister? You think somebody's going to marry you, is that it? Well, you're not the type that gets dates, let alone gets married. Nobody's going to notice you. And you have to talk for interviews, speak right up in front of the boss. Don't you know that? You're so dumb. Why do I waste my time on you?" Sniffling and snorting, I couldn't stop crying and talking at the same time. I kept wiping my nose on my arm, my sweater lost somewhere (probably not worn because my mother said to wear a sweater). It seemed as if I had spent my life in that basement, doing the worst thing I had yet done to another person. "I'm doing this for your own good," I said. "Don't you dare tell anyone I've been bad to you. Talk. Please talk." [19]

I was getting dizzy from the air I was gulping. Her sobs and my sobs were bouncing wildly off the tile, sometimes together, sometimes alternating. "I don't understand why you won't say just one word," I cried, clenching my teeth. My knees were shaking, and I hung on to her hair to stand up. Another time I'd stayed too late, I had to walk around two Negro kids who were bonking each other's head on the concrete. I went back later to see if the concrete had cracks in it. "Look. I'll give you something if you talk. I'll give you my pencil box. I'll buy you some candy. O.K.? What do you want? Tell me. Just say it and I'll give it to you. Just say, 'yes,' or, 'O.K.,' or 'Baby Ruth.'" But she didn't want anything. [20]

I had stopped pinching her cheek because I did not like the feel of her skin. I would go crazy if it came away in my hands. "I skinned her," I would have to confess. [21]

Suddenly I heard footsteps hurrying through the basement, and her sister ran into the lavatory calling her name. "Oh, there you are," I said. We've been waiting for you. I was only trying to teach her to talk. She wouldn't cooperate, though." Her sister went into one of [22] the stalls and got handfuls of toilet paper and wiped her off. Then we found my sister, and we walked home together. "Your family really ought to force her to speak," I advised all the way home. "You mustn't pamper her."

The world is sometimes just, and I spent the next eighteen months sick in bed with a mysterious illness. There was no pain and no symptoms, though the middle line in my left palm broke in two. Instead of starting junior high school, I lived like the Victorian recluses I read about. I had a rented hospital bed in the living room, where I watched soap operas on TV, and my family cranked me up and down. I saw no one but my family, who took good care of me. I could have no visitors, no other relatives, no villagers. My bed was against the west window, and I watched the seasons change the peach tree. I had a bell to ring for help. I used a bedpan. It was the best year and a half of my life. Nothing happened. 23

But one day my mother, the doctor, said, "You're ready to get up today. It's time to get up and go to school." I walked about outside to get my legs working, leaning on a staff I cut from the peach tree. The sky and trees, the sun were immense—no longer framed by a window, no longer grayed with a fly screen. I sat down on the sidewalk in amazement—the night, the stars. But at school I had to figure out again how to talk. I met again the poor girl I had tormented. She had not changed. She wore the same clothes, hair cut, and manner as when we were in elementary school, no make-up on the pink and white face, while the other Asian girls were starting to tape their eyelids. She continued to be able to read aloud. But there was hardly any reading aloud anymore, less and less as we got into high school. . . . 24

QUESTIONS FOR DISCUSSION

1 What is the impact of the first-person narration in "The Silent Girl"?

2 How have both girls been influenced by the cultural stereotypes of Asian women? Who are the ghosts that the narrator refers to? How does she feel about the ghosts?

3 In what ways are the two girls similar? How are they different? What precipitates the incident?

4 Why do you think the narrator loses control of herself? Do you think that the narrator was in some way trying to help the silent girl, or was she only being cruel? Why won't the silent girl give in to the narrator's bullying and speak?

5 What caused the narrator to have her mysterious illness? What helps her to recover?

IDEAS FOR WRITING

1   Write an essay about cultural stereotypes that you have had to struggle against in school. How have these experiences educated you?

2   Often the education that occurs outside of the classroom—in the cafeterias and halls, on the playground, in the lavatories—is more intense than the education that is taking place inside the classroom. Write an essay in which you discuss the relationships between the learning that goes on in classrooms and the learning that goes on on the school grounds. Draw your own conclusions.

Learning at School

Corla Hawkins

JONATHAN KOZOL

For over thirty years Jonathan Kozol (b. 1936) has written about impoverished children and spoken for their rights. After graduating from Harvard and studying in Britain as a Rhodes scholar, Kozol took his first teaching job at a segregated school in Boston, where he began to learn firsthand about the racism and corruption in public schools. Kozol won the National Book Award in 1967 for his searing account of public school life in Death at an Early Age. *He has written about the alternative school movement, middle-class education, adult illiteracy, and homelessness. His most widely read books include* Illiterate America *(1986),* Rachel and Her Children: Homeless Families in America *(1988), and* Amazing Grace: The Lives of Children and the Conscience of a Nation *(1995). The excerpt that follows is from* Savage Inequalities *(1992). While Kozol exposes the failure of public schools, he finds hope in the dedication of caring teachers.*

Even in the most unhappy schools there are certain classes that   1
stand out like little islands of excitement, energy and hope. One of
these classes is a combination fifth and sixth grade at Bethune, taught
by a woman, maybe 40 years of age, named Corla Hawkins.

The classroom is full of lively voices when I enter. The children are   2
at work, surrounded by a clutter of big dictionaries, picture books and
gadgets, science games and plants and colorful milk cartons, which
the teacher purchased out of her own salary. An oversized Van Gogh
collection, open to a print of a sunflower, is balanced on a table-ledge
next to a fish tank and a turtle tank. Next to the table is a rocking chair.
Handwritten signs are on all sides: "Getting to know you," "Keeping
you safe," and, over a wall that holds some artwork by the children,
"Mrs. Hawkins Academy of Fine Arts." Near the windows, the oversized
leaves of several wild-looking plants partially cover rows of novels,
math books, and a new World Book Encyclopedia. In the opposite
corner is a "Science Learning Board" that holds small packets which
contain bulb sockets, bulbs and wires, lenses, magnets, balance scales
and pliers. In front of the learning board is a microscope. Several rugs
are thrown around the floor. On another table are a dozen soda bottles
sealed with glue and lying sideways, filled with colored water.

The room looks like a cheerful circus tent. In the center of it all, within   3
the rocking chair, and cradling a newborn in her arms, is Mrs. Hawkins.

The 30 children in the class are seated in groups of six at five of what   4
she calls "departments." Each department is composed of six desks
pushed together to create a table. One of the groups is doing math,
another something they call "math strategy." A third is doing reading. Of

the other two groups, one is doing something they describe as "mathematics art"—painting composites of geometric shapes—and the other is studying "careers," which on this morning is a writing exercise about successful business leaders who began their lives in poverty. Near the science learning board a young-looking woman is preparing a new lesson that involves a lot of gadgets she has taken from a closet.

"This woman," Mrs. Hawkins tells me, "is a parent. She wanted to help me. So I told her, 'If you don't have somebody to keep your baby, bring the baby here. I'll be the mother. I can do it.'"   5

As we talk, a boy who wears big glasses brings his book to her and asks her what the word *salvation* means. She shows him how to sound it out, then tells him, "Use your dictionary if you don't know what it means." When a boy at the reading table argues with the boy beside him, she yells out, "You ought to be ashamed. You woke my baby."   6

After 15 minutes she calls out that it is time to change their tables. The children get up and move to new departments. As each group gets up to move to the next table, one child stays behind to introduce the next group to the lesson.   7

"This is the point of it," she says. "I'm teaching them three things. Number one: self-motivation. Number two: self-esteem. Number three: you help your sister and your brother. I tell them they're responsible for one another. I give no grades in the first marking period because I do not want them to be too competitive. Second marking period, you get your grade on what you've taught you neighbors at your table. Third marking period, I team them two-and-two. You get the same grade as your partner. Fourth marking period, I tell them, 'Every fish swims on its own.' But I wait a while for that. The most important thing for me is that they teach each other. . . .   8

"All this stuff"—she gestures at the clutter in the room—"I bought myself because it never works to order things through the school system. I bought the VCR. I bought the rocking chair at a flea market. I got these books here for ten cents a piece at a flea market. I bought that encyclopedia"—she points at the row of World Books—"so that they can do their research right here in this room."   9

I ask her if the class reads well enough to handle these materials. "Most of them can read some of these books. What they cannot, another child can read to them," she says.   10

"I tell the parents, 'Any time your child says, "I don't have no homework," call me up. Call me at home.' Because I give them homework every night and weekends too. Holidays I give them extra. Every child in this classroom has my phone."   11

Cradling the infant in her lap, she says, "I got to buy a playpen."   12

The bottles of colored water, she explains, are called "wave bottles." The children make them out of plastic soda bottles which they clean and fill with water and food coloring and seal with glue. She takes one in her hand and rolls it slowly to and fro. "It shows them how waves   13 form," she says. "I let them keep them at their desks. Some of them hold them in their hands while they're at work. It seems to calm them: seeing the water cloud up like a storm and then grow clear. . . .

"I take them outside every day during my teacher-break. On Saturdays we go to places like the art museum. Tuesdays, after school, I coach the drill team. Friday afternoons I tutor parents for their GED [high school equivalency exam]. If you're here this afternoon, I do the gospel choir." 14

When I ask about her own upbringing, she replies, "I went to school here in Chicago. My mother believed I was a 'gifted' child, but the system did not challenge me and I was bored at school. Fortunately one of my mother's neighbors was a teacher and she used to talk to me and help me after school. If it were not for her I doubt that I'd have thought that I could go to college. I promised myself I would return that favor." 15

At the end of class I go downstairs to see the principal, and then return to a second-floor room to see the gospel choir in rehearsal. When I arrive, they've already begun. Thirty-five children, ten of whom are boys, are standing in rows before a piano player. Next to the piano, Mrs. Hawkins stands and leads them through the words. The children range in age from sixth and seventh graders to three second graders and three tiny children, one of whom is Mrs. Hawkins's daughter, who are kindergarten pupils in the school. 16

They sing a number of gospel songs with Mrs. Hawkins pointing to each group—soprano, alto, bass—when it is their turn to join in. When they sing, "I love you, Lord," their voices lack the energy she wants. She interrupts and shouts at them, "Do you love Him? Do you?" They sing louder. The children look as if they're riveted to her directions. 17

"This next song," she says, "I dreamed about this. This song is my favorite." 18

The piano begins. The children start to clap their hands. When she gives the signal they begin to sing: 19

Clap your hands!
Stamp your feet!
Get on up
Out of your seats!
Help me
Lift 'em up, Lord!
Help me
Lift 'em up!

When a child she calls "Reverend Joe" does not come in at the right note, Mrs. Hawkins stops and says to him: "I thought you told me you were saved!" 20

The children smile. The boy called "Reverend Joe" stands up a little straighter. Then the piano starts again. The sound of children clap- 21

ping and then stamping with the music fills the room. Mrs. Hawkins
waves her arms. Then, as the children start, she also starts to sing.

Help me lift 'em up, Lord!
Help me lift 'em up!

There are wonderful teachers such as Corla Hawkins almost every-   22
where in urban schools, and sometimes a number of such teachers in
a single school. It is tempting to focus on these teachers and, by doing
this, to paint a hopeful portrait of the good things that go on under ad-
verse conditions. There is, indeed, a growing body of such writing; and
these books are sometimes very popular, because they are consoling.

The rationale behind much of this writing is that pedagogic prob-   23
lems in our cities are not chiefly matters of injustice, inequality or seg-
regation, but of insufficient information about teaching strategies: If we
could simply learn "what works" in Corla Hawkins's room, we'd then be
in a position to repeat this all over Chicago in every other system.

But what is unique in Mrs. Hawkins's classroom is not what she   24
does but who she is. Warmth and humor and contagious energy cannot be replicated and cannot be written into any standardized curriculum. If they could, it would have happened long ago; for
wonderful teachers have been heroized in books and movies for at
least three decades. And the problems of Chicago are, in any case, not
those of insufficient information. If Mrs. Hawkins's fellow fifth grade
teachers simply needed information, they could get it easily by walking 20 steps across the hall and visiting her room. The problems are
systemic: The number of teachers over 60 years of age in the Chicago
system is twice that of the teachers under 30. The salary scale, too low
to keep exciting, youthful teachers in the system, leads the city to rely
on low-paid subs, who represent more than a quarter of Chicago's
teaching force. "We have teachers," Mrs. Hawkins says, "who only
bother to come in three days a week. One of these teachers comes in
usually around nine-thirty. You ask her how she can expect the kids to
care about their education if the teacher doesn't even come until
nine-thirty. She answers you, 'It makes no difference. Kids like these
aren't going anywhere.' The school board thinks it's saving money on
the subs. I tell them, 'Pay now or pay later.'"

But even substitute teachers in Chicago are quite frequently in   25
short supply. On an average morning in Chicago, 5,700 children in 190
classrooms come to school to find they have no teacher. The number
of children who have no teachers on a given morning in Chicago's
public schools is nearly twice the student population of New Trier
High School in nearby Winnetka.

"We have been in this class a whole semester," says a 15-year-old at   26
Du Sable High, one of Chicago's poorest secondary schools, "and they
still can't find us a teacher."

A student in auto mechanics at Du Sable says he'd been in class for   27
16 weeks before he learned to change a tire. His first teacher quit at
the beginning of the year. Another teacher slept through most of the
semester. He would come in, the student says, and tell the students,
"You can talk. Just keep it down." He would soon be asleep.

"Let's be real," the student says. "Most of us ain't going to college. . . .   28
We could have used a class like this."

The shortage of teachers finds its parallel in a shortage of supplies.   29
A chemistry teacher at the school reports that he does not have
beakers, water, bunsen burners. He uses a popcorn popper as a substitute for a bunsen burner, and he cuts down plastic soda bottles to
make laboratory dishes.

Many of these schools make little effort to instruct their failing   30
students. "If a kid comes in not reading," says an English teacher at
Chicago's South Shore High, "he goes out not reading."

Another teacher at the school, where only 170 of 800 freshmen grad-   31
uate with their class, indicates that the dropout rate makes teaching
easier. "We lose all the dregs by the second year," he says.

"We're a general high school," says the head of counseling at   32
Chicago's Calumet High School. "We have second- and third-grade
readers. . . . We hope to do better, but we won't die if we don't."

At Bowen High School, on the South Side of Chicago, students have   33
two or three "study halls" a day, in part to save the cost of teachers.
"Not much studying goes on in study hall," a supervising teacher says.
"I let the students play cards. . . . I figure they might get some math
skills out of it."

At the Lathrop Elementary School, a short walk from the corner   34
lot where Dr. King resided in North Lawndale, there are no hoops on the
basketball court and no swings in the playground. For 21 years, according to the *Chicago Tribune*, the school has been without a library.
Library books, which have been piled and abandoned in the lunch
room of the school, have "sprouted mold," the paper says. Some years
ago the school received the standard reading textbooks out of sequence:
The second workbook in the reading program came to the school before
the first. The principal, uncertain what to do with the wrong workbook,
was told by school officials it was "all right to work backwards. . . ."

This degree of equanimity in failure, critics note, has led most   35
affluent parents in Chicago to avoid the public system altogether. The
school board president in 1989, although a teacher and administrator
in the system for three decades, did not send his children to the public
schools. Nor does Mayor Richard Daley, Jr., nor did any of the previous
four mayors who had school-age children.

"Nobody in his right mind," says one of the city's aldermen, "would   36
send [his] kids to public school."

Many suburban legislators representing affluent school districts use   37
terms such as "sinkhole" when opposing funds for Chicago's children.

"We can't keep throwing money," said Governor Thompson in 1988, "into a black hole."

The *Chicago Tribune* notes that, when this phrase is used, people 38
hasten to explain that it is not intended as a slur against the race of many of Chicago's children. "But race," says the *Tribune*, "never is far from the surface...."

QUESTIONS FOR DISCUSSION

1 Explain why you agree or disagree with Hawkins when she says, "The most important thing for me is that they teach each other." How does Hawkins encourage her students to work with one another? How does she create a strong sense of community in her classroom? Do you think a strong sense of community is essential if learning is to take place?

2 In Hawkins's class, "the room looks like a cheerful circus tent," and many different activities are taking place at the same time. In what ways are the energy level, atmosphere, and mood of a classroom important? Do you think children can learn in such a busy classroom setting? Explain.

3 What makes Corla Hawkins a successful teacher? Do you agree with Kozol when he claims that imitating what Corla Hawkins does with her students would not necessarily assure success for another teacher? How does he think that people learn to become good teachers?

4 According to this selection, what conditions in poor urban schools make learning almost impossible? Do children who attend school in affluent neighborhoods always have an advantage over poor children? What advantages might a child from a poor family have?

5 What solutions are implied by this selection? What hope, if any, does Kozol hold out for our children and our public schools?

IDEAS FOR WRITING

1 Write an essay about the teacher who has most influenced you. What type of relationship did this teacher establish with students in general and with you in particular? How did he or she teach? How was your classroom arranged? Why do you think this teacher was successful?

2 Discuss the quality of public schools in your community. What impact have they had on you, your family, your neighbors, and your friends? Propose several realistic ways in which public schools in your community could be improved.

How Male and Female Students Use Language Differently

DEBORAH TANNEN

*Deborah Tannen, a researcher into the different ways of using lan-
guage characteristic of women and men, has written two best-selling
books,* You Just Don't Understand: Women and Men in Conversation
(1990) and Talking from 9 to 5 *(1994). She has been a professor of
linguistics at Georgetown University since 1979. Tannen was born in
New York in 1945 and earned her Ph.D. from the University of California at Berkeley. Her writing demonstrates that men and women speak
different languages learned in childhood. In the selection that follows,
originally published in the* Chronicle of Higher Education *(June 1991),
Tannen proposes that teachers use both small- and large-group discussion to optimize learning in coeducational classrooms.*

When I researched and wrote my latest book, *You Just Don't Under-   1
stand: Women and Men in Conversation*, the furthest thing from my
mind was reevaluating teaching strategies. But that has been one of
the direct benefits of having written the book.

The primary focus of my linguistic research always has been the   2
language of everyday conversation. One facet of this is conversational
style: how different regional, ethnic, and class backgrounds, as well
as age and gender, result in different ways of using language to communicate. *You Just Don't Understand* is about the conversational
styles of women and men. As I gained more insight into typically male
and female ways of using language, I began to suspect some of the
causes of the troubling facts that women who go to single-sex schools
do better in later life, and that when young women sit next to young
men in classrooms, the males talk more. This is not to say that all men
talk in class, nor that no women do. It is simply that a greater percentage of discussion time is taken by men's voices.

The research of sociologist and anthropologists such as Janet Lever,   3
Marjorie Harness Goodwin, and Donna Eder has shown that girls and
boys learn to use language differently in their sex-separate peer
groups. Typically, a girl has a best friend with whom she sits and talks,
frequently telling secrets. It's the telling of secrets, the fact and the
way that they talk to each other, that makes them best friends. For
boys, activities are central: their best friends are the ones they do
things with. Boys also tend to play in larger groups that are hierarchical. High-status boys give orders and push low-status boys around.
So boys are expected to use language to seize center stage: by exhibit-
ing their skill, displaying their knowledge, and challenging and resisting challenges.

These patterns have stunning implications for classroom interac-   4
tion. Most faculty members assume that participating in class discussion is a necessary part of successful performance. Yet speaking in
a classroom is more congenial to boys' language experience than to
girls', since it entails putting oneself forward in front of a large group
of people, many of whom are strangers and at least one of whom is
sure to judge speakers' knowledge and intelligence by their verbal
display.

Another aspect of many classrooms that makes them more hos-   5
pitable to most men than to most women is the use of debate-like
formats as a learning tool. Our educational system, as Walter Ong
argues persuasively in his book *Fighting for Life* (Cornell University
Press, 1981), is fundamentally male in that the pursuit of knowledge is
believed to be achieved by ritual opposition: public display followed
by argument and challenge. Father Ong demonstrates that ritual opposition—what he calls "adversativeness" or "agonism"—is fundamental
to the way most males approach almost any activity. (Consider, for example, the little boy who shows he likes a little girl by pulling her braids
or shoving her.) But ritual opposition is antithetical to the way most
females learn and like to interact. It is not that females don't fight, but
that they don't fight for fun. They don't *ritualize* opposition.

Anthropologists working in widely disparate parts of the world   6
have found contrasting verbal rituals for women and men. Women in
completely unrelated cultures (for example, Greece and Bali) engage
in ritual laments: spontaneously produced rhyming couplets that express their pain, for example, over the loss of loved ones. Men do not
take part in laments. They have their own, very different verbal ritual:
a contest, a war of words in which they vie with each other to devise
clever insults.

When discussing these phenomena with a colleague, I commented   7
that I see these two styles in American conversation: many women
bond by talking about troubles, and many men bond by exchanging
playful insults and put-downs, and other sorts of verbal sparring. He
exclaimed: "I never thought of this, but that's the way I teach: I have
students read an article, and then I invite them to tear it apart. After
we've torn it to shreds, we talk about how to build a better model."

This contrasts sharply with the way I teach: I open the discussion   8
of readings by asking, "What did you find useful in this? What can
we use in our own theory building and our own methods?" I note
what I see as weaknesses in the author's approach, but I also point
out that the writer's discipline and purposes might be different from
ours. Finally, I offer personal anecdotes illustrating the phenomena
under discussion and praise students' anecdotes as well as their critical acumen.

These different teaching styles must make our classrooms wildly   9
different places and hospitable to different students. Male students

are more likely to be comfortable attacking the readings and might find the inclusion of personal anecdotes irrelevant and "soft." Women are more likely to resist discussion they perceive as hostile, and, indeed, it is women in my classes who are most likely to offer personal anecdotes.

A colleague who read my book commented that he had always   10
taken for granted that the best way to deal with students' comments is to challenge them; this, he felt it was self-evident, sharpens their minds and helps them develop debating skills. But he had noticed that women were relatively silent in his classes, so he decided to try beginning discussion with relatively open-ended questions and letting comments go unchallenged. He found, to his amazement and satisfaction, that more women began to speak up.

Though some of the women in his class clearly liked this better,   11
perhaps some of the men liked it less. One young man in my class wrote in a questionnaire about a history professor who gave students questions to think about and called on people to answer them: "He would then play devil's advocate . . . *i.e.*, he debated us. . . . That class *really* sharpened me intellectually. . . . We as students do need to know how to defend ourselves." This young man valued the experience of being attacked and challenged publicly. Many, if not most, women would shrink from such "challenge," experiencing it as public humiliation.

A professor at Hamilton College told me of a young man who was   12
upset because he felt that his class presentation had been a failure. The professor was puzzled because he had observed that class members had listened attentively and agreed with the student's observations. It turned out that it was this very agreement that the student interpreted as failure: since no one had engaged his ideas by arguing with him, he felt they had found them unworthy of attention.

So one reason men speak in class more than women is that many of   13
them find the "public" classroom setting more conducive to speaking, whereas most women are more comfortable speaking in private to a small group of people they know well. A second reason is that men are more likely to be comfortable with the debate-like form that discussion may take. Yet another reason is the different attitudes toward speaking in class that typify women and men.

Students who speak frequently in class, many of whom are men,   14
assume that it is their job to think of contributions and try to get the floor to express them. But many women monitor their participation not only to get the floor but to avoid getting it. Women students in my class tell me that if they have spoken up once or twice, they hold back for the rest of the class because they don't want to dominate. If they have spoken a lot one week, they will remain silent the next. These different ethics of participation are, of course, unstated, so those who

speak freely assume that those who remain silent have nothing to say, and those who are reining themselves assume that the big talkers are selfish and hoggish.

When I looked around my classes, I could see these differing ethics and habits at work. For example, my graduate class in analyzing conversation had twenty students, eleven women and nine men. Of the men, four were foreign students: two Japanese, one Chinese, and one Syrian. With the exception of the three Asian men, all the men spoke in class at least occasionally. The biggest talker in the class was a woman, but there were also five women who never spoke at all, only one of whom was Japanese. I decided to try something different.   15

I broke the class into small groups to discuss the issues raised in the readings and to analyze their own conversational transcripts. I devised three ways of dividing the students into groups: one by the degree program they were in, one by gender, and one by conversational style, as closely as I could guess it. This meant that when the class was grouped according to conversational style, I put Asian students together, fast talkers together, and quiet students together. The class split into groups six times during the semester, so they met in each grouping twice. I told students to regard the groups as examples of interactional data and to note the different ways they participated in the different groups. Toward the end of the term, I gave them a questionnaire asking about their class and group participation.   16

I could see plainly from my observation of the groups at work that women who never opened their mouths in class were talking away in the small groups. In fact, the Japanese woman commented that she found it particularly hard to the all-woman group she was in because "I was overwhelmed by how talkative the female students were in the female-only group." This is particularly revealing because it highlights that the same person who can be "oppressed" into silence in one context can become the talkative "oppressor" in another. No one's conversational style is absolute; everyone's style changes in response to the context and others' styles.   17

Some of the students (seven) said they preferred the same-gender groups; others preferred the same-style groups. In answer to the question "Would you have liked to speak in class more often than you did?" six of the seven who said yes were women; the one man was Japanese. Most startlingly, this response did not come only from quiet women; it came from women who had indicated that they had spoken in class never, rarely, sometimes, and often. Of the eleven students who said the amount they had spoken was fine, seven were men. Of the four women who checked "fine," two added qualifications indicating it wasn't completely fine: One wrote in "maybe more," and one wrote, "I have an urge to participate but often feel I should have something more interesting/relevant/wonderful/intelligent to say!!"   18

I counted my experiment a success. Everyone in the class found the   19
small groups interesting, and no one indicated he or she would have
preferred that the class not break into groups. Perhaps more instruc-
tive, however, was the fact that the experience of breaking into groups,
and of talking about participation in class, raised everyone's awareness
about classroom participation. After we had talked about it, some of
the quietest women in the class made a few voluntary contributions,
though sometimes I had to ensure their participation by interrupting
students who were exuberantly speaking out.

Americans are often proud that they discount the significance of   20
cultural differences: "We are all individuals," many people boast.
Ignoring such issues as gender and ethnicity becomes a source of
pride: "I treat everyone the same." But treating people the same is not
equal treatment if they are not the same.

The classroom is a different environment for those who feel comfort-   21
able putting themselves forward in a group than it is for those who find
the prospect of doing so chastening, or even terrifying. When a professor asks, "Are there any questions?" students who can formulate state-
ments the fastest have the greatest opportunity to respond. Those who
need significant time to do so have not really been given a chance at all,
since by the time they are ready to speak, someone else has the floor.

In a class where some students speak out without raising hands,   22
those who feel they must raise their hands and wait to be recognized
do not have equal opportunity to speak. Telling them to feel free to
jump in will not make them feel free; one's sense of timing, of one's
rights and obligations in a classroom, are automatic, learned over
years of interaction. They may be changed over time, with motivation
and effort, but they cannot be changed on the spot. And everyone as-
sumes his or her own way is best. When I asked my students how the
class could be changed to make it easier for them to speak more, the
most talkative woman said she would prefer it if no one had to raise
hands, and a foreign student said he wished people would raise their
hands and wait to be recognized.

My experience in this class has convinced me that small-group in-   23
teraction should be part of any class that is not a small seminar. I also
am convinced that having the students become observers of their
own interaction is a crucial part of their education. Talking about
ways of talking in class makes students aware that their ways of talking affect other students, that the motivations they impute to others
may not truly reflect others' motives, and that the behaviors they
assume to be self-evidently right are not universal norms.

The goal of complete equal opportunity in class may not be attain-   24
able, but realizing that one monolithic classroom-participation structure is not equal opportunity is itself a powerful motivation to find
more-diverse methods to serve diverse students—and every classroom is diverse.

QUESTIONS FOR DISCUSSION

1   Why does Tannen think that girls and boys learn to value talking for different reasons? Why does Tannen think that boys and girls, men and women, feel differently about contributing to classroom discussions? Explain why you agree or disagree with Tannen's assertions.

2   Explain Tannen's claim in paragraph 20, "But treating people the same is not equal treatment if they are not the same." Discuss whether you agree or disagree with Tannen's point, citing your own experiences.

3   Tannen believes that students learn more when they work in small groups and when they also make themselves aware of the ways in which the males and females in the group talk to one another and how this affects other students. Explain why you agree or disagree with her.

4   Discuss the issue of how men and women react to class discussion with a small group of your peers. Report your findings back to the whole class. Then have the class compile the various groups' findings and discuss what you have learned from the small- and large-group discussion.

5   Tannen uses a variety of types of support for her assertions and conclusions. Cite several examples of different types of evidence that she uses effectively. Explain why the evidence is or is not persuasive.

IDEAS FOR WRITING

1   Referring to your own learning experiences, write an essay that supports or refutes Tannen's assertions about how men and women communicate with one another in classrooms. Conclude by proposing ways in which communication between males and females in classroom situations could be improved.

2   Do some research into how gender issues affect learning in the classroom. Write an essay that discusses what you have uncovered through your research.

Possible Lives

MIKE ROSE

Mike Rose (b. 1944) grew up in East Los Angeles and earned his Ph.D. in educational psychology. Before joining the faculty at the UCLA Graduate School of Education and Information Studies and the UCLA Writing Program, Rose worked as a teacher in poor neighborhoods in East Los Angeles. Rose established his authority as a spokesperson for underprepared and poor students in his best-selling book Lives on The Boundary *(1989), which explores the injustices that our educational system perpetuates through tracking. The selection that follows is from his most recent book,* Possible Lives: The Promise of Public Education in America *(1995). As you read the selection, think about the different reasons Rose gives for maintaining hope for our public educational system.*

The exit from the Warriors' stadium led back through the Tuba City, car light, lights from trucks, streetlights, moonlight over the roads that continued a journey I had begun three-and-a-half years before, trying to fashion a response to the loss of faith in our public schools. I was looking for a language of possibility, an imagery to spark our imagination. It was a wonderful trip, one many could take, full of revealing conversation and the pleasure of land—Happy Jack Road, Holy Moses Wash—a journey of surprise and resonance.

The search led outward, across landscapes—urban and rural—that were new to me, across the immensity of this country and its remarkable particularity: snow falling on a creek, a pasture, a frame schoolhouse; a block of brick storefronts—its mix of dry goods, melons, language, fish on ice, apples, information, opportunity; billowing smokestacks jutting out of pine; the desert after rainfall; empty mills where rivers cross, thick with pain and goldenrod; a train whistle through the hollows; cornfields symmetrical on a page and in the clear air below.

And, as is the case with so many journeys, this one led inward as well. I had been studying schools for much of my adult life, had been trying to understand how they enhanced the lives of students or diminished them. Most of that work was located in and around the LA Basin. For all its bewildering complication, Los Angeles was familiar territory, home. Those trips to Calexico, to Baltimore, to Eastern Kentucky, to a nation within a nation in northern Arizona brought forth new cultural practices, new languages, new gestures. I was fortunate to have been escorted into so many classrooms, so many homes, to have been guided into the everyday events of the communities I visited, for the invitation eased the unfamiliarity and discomfort that could have been present on all sides. What I experienced was a kind of awe at our variety, yet an intimate regard, a handshake on the corner, a sense of shared humanity. The complex interplay of difference and commonality. What began as a search for a fresh language of educational critique and invention became, as well, a search for what is best in this country—realized infrequently, threatened at every turn—but there to be summoned, possible in the public domain, there to instruct a traveler settling into a seat in the corner of a classroom.

It was, in many ways, an odd time to be on such a journey. The country was in the grip of a nasty reactive politics, a volatile mix of anger and anxiety. And people of all political persuasion were withdrawing from engagement with the public sphere. It was time of economic and moral cocooning. The question for me—framed in terms of public schools, our pre-eminent institution—was how to generate a hopeful vision in a time of bitterness and lost faith, and further, how to do that in a way that holds simultaneously to what educational philosopher David Purpel calls "the interlocking and interdependent hinges" of criticism and creativity. How to sharpen awareness of injustice and incompetence, how to maintain the skeptic's acuity, yet nurture the ability to imagine the possible and act from hope.

The journey was odd for me in another way, considering my own teaching history. My work in the classroom has mostly been with people whom our schools, public and private, have failed: working-class and immigrant students, students from nonmainstream linguistic and cultural backgrounds, students of all backgrounds who didn't fit a curriculum or timetable or definition of achievement and were thereby categorized in some way as different or deficient. There are, as we have seen along this journey, long-standing social and cultural reasons for this failure in our schools, tangled, disturbing histories of discrimination, skewed perception, and protection of privilege.

And yet there were these rooms. Vital, varied, they were providing a powerful education for the children in them, many of whom were members of the very groups defined as inferior in times past and, not infrequently, in our ungenerous present. What I began to see—and it took the accumulation of diverse classrooms to help me see it—was that these classrooms, in addition to whatever else we may understand about them, represented a dynamic, at times compromised and contested, strain in American educational history: a faith in the capacity of people, a drive toward equality and opportunity, a belief in the intimate link between mass education and a free society. These rooms were embodiments of the democratic ideal. To be sure, this democratic impulse has been undercut and violated virtually since its first articulation. Thomas Jefferson's proposal to the Virginia legislature for three years of free public schooling, for example, excluded the commonwealth's significant number of enslaved Black children. But it has been advanced, realized in daily classroom life by a long history of educators working both within the mainstream and outside it, challenging it through workingmen's organizations, women's groups, Black schools, appropriating the ideal, often against political and economic resistance, to their own emancipatory ends.

The teachers I visited were working within that rich tradition. They 7 provided example after different example of people doing public intellectual work in institutional settings, using the power of the institution to realize democratic goals for the children in their charge, and finessing, negotiating, subverting institutional power when it blocked the realization of those goals. At a time of profound disillusionment with public institutional life, these people were, in their distinct ways, creating the conditions for children to develop lives of possibility.

My hope is that these classrooms will help us imagine—and, in 8 imagining, struggle to achieve—what schools in the public domain, and perhaps a range of public institutions, can be.

Whether or not an institution is democratic is often determined by 9 procedural criteria. Do members have a vote, input into policy, a place at the table? These concerns are important, of course, but considered alone, or primarily, can lead to reductive definitions of democracy, democracy as procedure, as a set of rules. My visits led me to be more interested in the *experience* of democracy, the phenomenology of it. What did it feel like to be in those classrooms in Watts, on the South Side, in the Eastern Coal Field, in Hattiesburg and Missoula, in Calexico and Tucson? If we can situate ourselves within that experience, we may come to understand on many levels, not just the definitional and formal, what schooling for all in a democratic society can be and how we can meaningfully talk about it.

The first thing to say about the rooms I visited is that they created a 10 sense of safety. There was physical safety, which for some children in some environments is a real consideration. But there was also safety from insult and diminishment: "They don't make fun of you if you mess up," said the middle school student in Chicago. And there was safety to take risks, to push beyond what you can comfortably do at present, "coaxing our thinking along," as one of Steve Gilbert's students put it, "bringing out our best interpretive abilities."

Intimately related to safety is respect, a word I heard frequently during my travels. From what I could tell, it meant many things, operated 11 on many levels: fair treatment, decency, an absence of intimidation, and, beyond the realm of individual civility, a respect for the history, the language and culture of the peoples represented in the classroom. Surveying the images of Mexican and Mexican-American history on Carlos Jimenez's walls and bulletin boards, a Chicano student exclaimed, "This room is something *positive*. As you walk around, you say, 'Hey, we're somebody!'" Respect also has an intellectual dimension. As New York principal Louis Delgado put it, "It's not just about being polite—even the curriculum has to convey respect. [It] has to be challenging enough that it's respectful." It's interesting that virtually all of our current discussions of academic standards are framed either in the quasi-technical language of assessment and accountability or as a lament for diminished performance. There could be a whole other discussion of standards in a language of expectation, respect, and democratic theory.

Talking about safety and respect leads to a consideration of authority. Most discussions of authority in the classroom involve either a teacher's "management" style (one common treatment, for example, contrasts an authoritarian with a democratic style) or the degree to which a teacher involves students in making decisions about what will be taught and how the class will be run. While none of the teachers I observed could be categorized as authoritarian, I did see a range of classroom management styles, and while some teachers involved students in determining the rules of classroom conduct and gave them significant responsibility to provide the class its direction, others came with curriculum and codes of conduct fairly well in place.

But two things seemed to hold across classrooms. First, a teacher's authority came from multiple sources—knowledge, care, the construction of safe and respectful space, solidarity with students' background—rather than solely from age or role. Though there were times when our teachers asserted authority in a direct and unilateral way, in general, authority was not expressed or experienced as a blunt exercise of power. As one of Stephanie Terry's first-graders put it, "She doesn't fuss a lot."

The second thing to note was that even in classrooms that were run in a relatively traditional manner, authority was distributed. In various ways, students contributed to the flow of events, shaped the direction of discussion, became authorities of their own experience and on the work they were doing. Think of Stephanie Terry's students reporting on their observations of the tree frog and hermit crab and Michelle Taigue's Navajo and Hopi students explaining slang and dialect on the reservation. There were multiple pathways of authority, multiple opportunities for members of the class to assume authority. And since authority and the generation of knowledge are intimately connected—those who can speak affect what is known—there were multiple opportunities to shape the knowledge emerging in the classroom.

These classrooms, then, were places of expectation and responsibility. Teachers took students seriously as intellectual and social beings. Young people had to work hard, think things through, come to terms with each other—and there were times when such effort took a student to his or her limits. "They looked at us in disbelief," said New York principal Haven Henderson, "when we told them they were intellectuals." The teachers we met assumed that a small society of achievement and civic behavior could flourish. "All children," said Evangelina

Jones in Calexico, "have minds and souls and have the ability to participate fully in society." It is important to note that such assumptions were realized through a range of supports, guides, and structures: from the way teachers organized curriculum and invited and answered questions, to the means of assistance they and their aides provided (tutoring, conferences, written and oral feedback), to the various ways they encouraged peer support and assistance, to the atmosphere they created in the room—which takes us back to considerations of safety and respect. These classrooms required thought, participation, effort— they were places where you did things—but not without mechanisms to aid involvement and achievement. Such aid to participation should be a defining quality of public institutions in a democracy.

This mix of expectation, responsibility, and assistance established   16 the conditions for students like the young woman in Mark Hall's Graphic Arts Lab in Pasadena to say, "I'm just learning all this. I can't wait to get really proficient at it." Or for the child in Calexico, engaged with an exercise on the telling of time, to implore Elena Castro to "make [the problems] harder." Earlier, I suggested that there could be in our country an alternative discussion on standards, one that involved expectation, respect, and democratic theory. Yvonne Hutchinson, the middle school teacher from Watts, offered one direction such a discussion might take:

> Teachers will say either "we can't lower our standards" or "this poor child is reading below grade level, so I'll need a third- or fourth-grade book." But what you need to do is find a way to make that eighth-grade book *accessible.* You have to respect the child . . . We get so busy looking at children in terms of labels that we fail to look for their *potential*—and to demand that kids live up to that potential. Children can tell right off those people who believe in them and those who patronize them. . . . They rise to whatever expectations are set. They rise or fail to rise. And when they rise, they can sometimes rise to great heights.

The students I talked to, from primary-grade children to graduat-   17 ing seniors, each in their own way, had the sense that these classrooms were salutatory places, places that felt good to be in, places that honored their best interests. "They really care about you," that student in Mark Hall's lab said of the Graphic Arts Academy. "It's like we're a family." Discussing difficult times in making their video, two students recalled Bell High School teacher Larry Stone's encouragement: "Girls, you have to do this . . . It'll work out. I believe in you." Calling Michelle Smith, of the COMETS program in Chicago, a "good teacher," a student explained that "she's teaching us how to do things we couldn't do before." "Math'll take you a long way in life," said an Algebra Project student in Hollandale, Mississippi. There was variation in the way it was experienced and expressed—nurturance, social cohesion, the fostering of competence, a sense of growth, a feeling of opportunity, futurity—but there was among the students I met a common recognition of concern and benefit.

The foregoing characteristics combined to create vital public space. 18 The rooms I visited felt alive. People were learning things, both cognitive and social, and doing things, individually and collectively, making contributions, connecting ideas, generating knowledge. To be sure, not everyone was engaged. And everyone, students and teachers, had bad days. But overall these classrooms were exciting places to be, places of reflection and challenge, of deliberation and expression, of quiet work and public presentation. People were encouraged to be smart. "I wanted to feel the challenge of tough courses," said Carlos Jimenez's student about electives like Mexican-American history. "I think I came to understand," said Lois Rodger's student after completing a video project on Camp Sister Spirit, "something about the fear behind prejudice." "[Rick Takagaki's] classes made me realize I needed to go experience things," observed a University High student in Los Angeles. These young people were acting as agents in their own development. And that agency became an essential force in sustaining the classroom. The work they were doing had an effect beyond itself.

In an important post-revolutionary essay on education, the 19 eighteenth-century journalist Samuel Harrison Smith wrote that the free play of intelligence was central to a democracy, and that individual intellectual growth was intimately connected to broad-scale intellectual development, to the "general diffusion of knowledge." To a significant degree, the occasion and energy for intellectual growth in these classrooms came from engagement with others, often over a common problem. Consider Aleta Sullivan's human anatomy and physiology students trying to find a solution to their blood-antigen experiment, or Bette Ford's students, also at Hattiesburg High, struggling to convey to an audience of children the complex legacy of sharecropping, or Michelle Taigue's students in Tucson trying to render in a videoplay the tension between White, urban education and the social fabric of reservation life.

Smith celebrated "the improvement of the mind and the collision 20 of mind with mind." As a number of contemporary critics of our public schools and of the larger public sphere have noted, what Smith referred to as "the general diffusion of knowledge" has been restricted in our country, and many voices remain silent. If we consider these rooms to be miniature public spheres or preparatory arenas for civic life, then it is essential to note how the formation of intellectually safe and respectful space, the distribution of authority and responsibility, the maintenance of high expectations and the means to attain them—how all this is essential to the development of the intelligence of a people.

QUESTIONS FOR DISCUSSION

1   In what ways are Rose's visits to the various classrooms both outward and inward journeys?

2   Why does Rose believe that American educators can overcome the failures of the past, "the disturbing histories of discrimination . . . and protections of privilege"?

3   Why is Rose more interested in the experience of democracy than the procedures of democracy? How does he connect effective education and democracy?

4   Why are safety and respect necessary components of a democratic classroom? Why was it important that the authority in these successful classrooms came from both students and teachers?

5   What did you learn about the meaning and experience of a democratic education from reading this selection? Do you agree with Rose that learning comes through engagement with a problem? Have you been in classrooms that are "democratic" in the sense in which Rose uses the term?

IDEAS FOR WRITING

1   Write an essay in which you contrast Rose's and Hirsch's assumptions about what should be taught and what constitutes an educational experience. With which of these educators do you most agree?

2   Write an essay about the most vital classroom in which you have been a student. Describe the teacher's approach, the classroom setting, the rules and social dynamics. Why was the teacher's approach effective? Compare and contrast what Rose considers the necessary ingredients for a successful learning experience with the assumptions that supported your own classroom experiences.

Learning and Diversity

Graduation

MAYA ANGELOU

Maya Angelou is a poet and memoirist who has read from her works and lectured all over the world. Born in 1928, she was raised in Stamps, Arkansas, by her grandmother, a storekeeper and community leader. Angelou is currently a Reynolds Professor of American Studies at Wake Forest University in North Carolina. I Know Why the Caged Bird Sings *(1970) opens her autobiography, which continues in* Gather Together in My Name *(1974),* Swingin' and Gettin' Merry Like Christmas *(1976), and* The Heart of a Woman *(1981). Angelou's memoirs most often reflect upon the impact of poverty and racism on the black community, as well as upon those moments of joy, insight, and creative expression that sometimes can ease the pain of oppression. Angelou, who has written five collections of poetry, was the first woman and African American to read at a presidential inauguration: She read her poem "On the Pulse of Morning" at President Clinton's first inauguration on January 20, 1993. Her recent work,* Wouldn't Take Nothing for My Journey Now *(1993), became a bestseller upon publication. In the following selection, excerpted from the first book of her memoir, Angelou gives us a vivid account of the treatment of African American high school students before World War II.*

The children in Stamps trembled visibly with anticipation. Some   1
adults were excited too, but to be certain the whole young population
had come down with graduation epidemic. Large classes were graduating from both the grammar school and the high school. Even those
who were years removed from their own day of glorious release were
anxious to help with preparations as a kind of dry run. The junior
students who were moving into the vacating classes' chairs were
tradition-bound to show their talents for leadership and management.
They strutted through the school and around the campus exerting
pressure on the lower grades. Their authority was so new that occasionally if they pressed a little too hard it had to be overlooked. After all,
next term was coming, and it never hurt a sixth grader to have a play
sister in the eighth grade, or a tenth-year student to be able to call a
twelfth grader Bubba. So all was endured in a spirit of shared understanding. But the graduating classes themselves were the nobility. Like
travelers with exotic destinations on their minds, the graduates were re-
markably forgetful. They came to school without their books, or tablets,
or even pencils. Volunteers fell over themselves to secure replacements
for the missing equipment. When accepted, the willing workers might
or might not be thanked, and it was of no importance to the pregrad-
uation rites. Even teachers were respectful of the now quiet and aging

seniors, and tended to speak to them, if not as equals, as beings only slightly lower than themselves. After tests were returned and grades given, the student body, which acted like an extended family, knew who did well, who excelled, and what piteous ones had failed.

Unlike the white school, Lafayette County Training School distin-   2
guished itself by having neither lawn, nor hedges, nor tennis court, nor climbing ivy. Its two buildings (main classrooms, the grade school, and home economics) were set on a dirt hill with no fence to limit either its boundaries or those of bordering farms. There was a large expanse to the left of the school which was used alternately as a baseball diamond or a basketball court. Rusty hoops on the swaying poles represented the permanent recreational equipment, although bats and balls could be borrowed from the P.E. teacher if the borrower was qualified and if the diamond wasn't occupied.

Over this rocky area relieved by a few shady tall persimmon trees   3
the graduating class walked. The girls often held hands and no longer bothered to speak to the lower students. There was a sadness about them, as if this old world was not their home and they were bound for higher ground. The boys, on the other hand, had become more friendly, more outgoing. A decided change from the closed attitude they projected while studying for finals. Now they seemed not ready to give up the old school, the familiar paths and classrooms. Only a small percentage would be continuing on to college—one of the South's A & M (agricultural and mechanical) schools, which trained Negro youths to be carpenters, farmers, handymen, masons, maids, cooks, and baby nurses. Their future rode heavily on their shoulders, and blinded them to the collective joy that had pervaded the lives of the boys and girls in the grammar school graduating class.

Parents who could afford it had ordered new shoes and ready-   4
made clothes for themselves from Sears and Roebuck or Montgomery Ward. They also engaged the best seamstresses to make the floating graduating dresses and to cut down secondhand pants which would be pressed to a military slickness for the important event.

Oh, it was important, all right. Whitefolks would attend the cere-   5
mony, and two or three would speak of God and home, and the Southern way of life, and Mrs. Parsons, the principal's wife, would play the graduation march while the lower-grade graduates paraded down the aisles and took their seats below the platform. The high school seniors would wait in empty classrooms to make their dramatic entrance.

In the Store I was the person of the moment. The birthday girl. The   6
center. Bailey[1] had graduated the year before, although to do so he had had to forfeit all pleasures to make up for his lost time in Baton Rouge.

---

[1]The author's brother. The children help out in their grandmother's store. [Ed.]

My class was wearing butter-yellow piqué dresses, and Momma   7
launched out on mine. She smocked the yoke into tiny crisscrossing
puckers, then shirred the rest of the bodice. Her dark fingers ducked in
and out of the lemony cloth as she embroidered raised daisies around
the hem. Before she considered herself finished she had added a
crocheted cuff on the puff sleeves, and a pointy crocheted collar.

I was going to be lovely. A walking model of all the various styles of   8
fine hand sewing and it didn't worry me that I was only twelve years old
and merely graduating from the eighth grade. Besides, many teachers
in Arkansas Negro schools had only that diploma and were licensed to
impart wisdom.

The days had become longer and more noticeable. The faded beige   9
of former times had been replaced with strong and sure colors. I
began to see my classmates' clothes, their skin tones, and the dust
that waved off pussy willows. Clouds that lazed across the sky were
objects of great concern to me. Their shiftier shapes might have held
a message that in my new happiness and with a little bit of time I'd
soon decipher. During that period I looked at the arch of heaven so
religiously my neck kept a steady ache. I had taken to smiling more
often, and my jaws hurt from the unaccustomed activity. Between the
two physical sore spots, I suppose I could have been uncomfortable,
but that was not the case. As a member of the winning team (the graduating class of 1940) I had outdistanced unpleasant sensations by miles.
I was headed for the freedom of open fields.

Youth and social approval allied themselves with me and we tram-   10
meled memories of slights and insults. The wind of our swift passage
remodeled my features. Lost tears were pounded to mud and then
to dust. Years of withdrawal were brushed aside and left behind, as
hanging ropes of parasitic moss.

My work alone had awarded me a top place and I was going to   11
be one of the first called in the graduating ceremonies. On the classroom blackboard, as well as on the bulletin board in the auditorium,
there were blue stars and white stars and red stars. No absences, no
tardinesses, and my academic work was among the best of the year. I
could say the preamble to the Constitution even faster than Bailey. We
timed ourselves often: "WethepeopleoftheUnitedStatesinordertoform-
amoreperfectunion . . ." I had memorized the Presidents of the United
States from Washington to Roosevelt in chronological as well as alpha-
betical order.

My hair pleased me too. Gradually the black mass had lengthened   12
and thickened, so that it kept at last to its braided pattern, and I didn't
have to yank my scalp off when I tried to comb it.

Louise and I had rehearsed the exercises until we tired ourselves.   13
Henry Reed was class valedictorian. He was a small, very black boy
with hooded eyes, a long, broad nose, and an oddly shaped head. I
had admired him for years because each term he and I vied for the

best grades in our class. Most often he bested me, but instead of being disappointed I was pleased that we shared top places between us. Like many Southern Black children, he lived with his grandmother, who was as strict as Momma and as kind as she knew how to be. He was courteous, respectful, and soft-spoken to elders, but on the playground he chose to play the roughest games. I admired him. Anyone, I reckoned, sufficiently afraid or sufficiently dull could be polite. But to be able to operate at the top level with both adults and children was admirable.

His valedictory speech was entitled "To Be or Not to Be." The rigid 14 tenth-grade teacher had helped him to write it. He'd been working on the dramatic stresses for months.

The weeks until graduation were filled with heady activities. A group 15 of small children were to be presented in a play about buttercups and daisies and bunny rabbits. They could be heard throughout the building practicing their hops and their little songs that sounded like silver bells. The older girls (nongraduates, of course) were assigned the task of making refreshments for the night's festivities. A tangy scent of ginger, cinnamon, nutmeg, and chocolate wafted around the home economics building as the budding cooks made samples for themselves and their teachers.

In every corner of the workshop, axes and saws split fresh timber as 16 the woodshop boys made sets and stage scenery. Only the graduates were left out of the general bustle. We were free to sit in the library at the back of the building or look in quite detachedly, naturally, on the measures being taken for our event.

Even the minister preached on graduation the Sunday before. His 17 subject was, "Let your light so shine that men will see your good works and praise your Father, Who is in Heaven." Although the sermon was purported to be addressed to us, he used the occasion to speak to backsliders, gamblers, and general ne'er-do-wells. But since he had called our names at the beginning of the service we were mollified.

Among Negroes the tradition was to give presents to children going 18 only from one grade to another. How much more important this was when the person was graduating at the top of the class. Uncle Willie and Momma had sent away for a Mickey Mouse watch like Bailey's. Louise gave me four embroidered handkerchiefs. (I gave her three crocheted doilies.) Mrs. Sneed, the minister's wife, made me an underskirt to wear for graduation, and nearly every customer gave me a nickel or maybe even a dime with the instruction "Keep on moving to higher ground," or some such encouragement.

Amazingly the great day finally dawned and I was out of bed before 19 I knew it. I threw open the back door to see it more clearly, but Momma said, "Sister, come away from that door and put your robe on."

I hoped the memory of that morning would never leave me. Sunlight 20 was itself still young, and the day had none of the insistence maturity would bring it in a few hours. In my robe and barefoot in the backyard, under cover of going to see about my new beans, I gave myself up to the gentle warmth and thanked God that no matter what evil I had done in my life He had allowed me to live to see this day. Somewhere in my fatalism I had expected to die, accidentally, and never have the chance to walk up the stairs in the auditorium and gracefully receive my heard-earned diploma. Out of God's merciful bosom I had won reprieve.

Bailey came out in his robe and gave me a box wrapped in Christ-   21
mas paper. He said he had saved his money for months to pay for it. It felt like a box of chocolates, but I knew Bailey wouldn't save money to buy candy when we had all we could want under our noses.

He was as proud of the gift as I. It was a soft-leather-bound copy of   22
a collection of poems by Edgar Allan Poe, or, as Bailey and I called him, "Eap." I turned to "Annabel Lee" and we walked up and down the garden rows, the cool dirt between our toes, reciting the beautifully sad lines.

Momma made a Sunday breakfast although it was only Friday.   23
After we finished the blessing, I opened my eyes to find the watch on my plate. It was a dream of a day. Everything went smoothly and to my credit. I didn't have to be reminded or scolded for anything. Near evening I was too jittery to attend to chores, so Bailey volunteered to do all before his bath.

Days before, we had made a sign for the Store and as we turned out   24
the lights Momma hung the cardboard over the doorknob. It read clearly: CLOSED. GRADUATION.

My dress fitted perfectly and everyone said that I looked like a sun-   25
beam in it. On the hill, going toward the school, Bailey walked behind with Uncle Willie, who muttered, "Go on, Ju." He wanted him to walk ahead with us because it embarrassed him to have to walk so slowly. Bailey said he'd let the ladies walk together, and the men would bring up the rear. We all laughed, nicely.

Little children dashed by out of the dark like fireflies. Their crepe-   26
paper dresses and butterfly wings were not made for running and we heard more than one rip, dryly, and the regretful "uh uh" that followed.

The school blazed without gaiety. The windows seemed cold and   27
unfriendly from the lower hill. A sense of ill-fated timing crept over me, and if Momma hadn't reached for my hand I would have drifted back to Bailey and Uncle Willie, and possibly beyond. She made a few slow jokes about my feet getting cold, and tugged me along to the now-strange building.

Around the front steps, assurance came back. There were my fellow   28
"greats," the graduating class. Hair brushed back, legs oiled, new dresses and pressed pleats, fresh pocket handkerchiefs and little handbags, all homesewn. Oh, we were up to snuff, all right. I joined my comrades and didn't even see my family go in to find seats in the crowded auditorium.

The school band struck up a march and all classes filed in as had been rehearsed. We stood in front of our seats, as assigned, and on a signal from the choir director, we sat. No sooner had this been accomplished than the band started to play the national anthem. We rose again and sang the song, after which we recited the pledge of allegiance. We remained standing for a brief minute before the choir director and the principal signaled to us, rather desperately I thought, to take our seats. The command was so unusual that our carefully rehearsed smooth-running machine was thrown off. For a full minute we fumbled for our chairs and bumped into each other awkwardly. Habits change or solidify under pressure, so in our state of nervous tension we had been ready to follow our usual pattern: the American National Anthem, then the pledge of allegiance, then the song every Black person I knew called the Negro National Anthem. All done in the same key, with the same passion and most often standing on the same foot. 29

Finding my seat at last, I was overcome with a presentiment of worse things to come. Something unrehearsed, unplanned, was going to happen, and we were going to be made to look bad. I distinctly remember being explicit in the choice of pronoun. It was "we," the graduating class, the unit, that concerned me then. 30

The principal welcomed "parents and friends" and asked the Baptist minister to lead us in prayer. His invocation was brief and punchy, and for a second I thought we were getting back on the high road to right action. When the principal came back, however, his voice had changed. Sounds always affected me profoundly and the principal's voice was one of my favorites. During assembly it melted and lowed weakly into the audience. It had not been my plan to listen to him, but my curiosity was piqued and I straightened up to give him my attention. 31

He was talking about Booker T. Washington, our "late great leader," who said we can be as close as the fingers on the hand, etc. . . . Then he said a few vague things about friendship and the friendship of kindly people to those less fortunate than themselves. With that his voice nearly faded, thin, away. Like a river diminishing to a stream and then to a trickle. But he cleared his throat and said, "Our speaker tonight, who is also our friend, came from Texarkana to deliver the commencement address, but due to the irregularity of the train schedule, he's going to, as they say, 'speak and run.'" He said that we understood and wanted the man to know that we were most grateful for the time he was able to give us and then something about how we were willing always to adjust to another's program, and without more ado—"I give you Mr. Edward Donleavy." 32

Not one but two white men came through the door offstage. The shorter one walked to the speaker's platform, and the tall one moved over to the center seat and sat down. But that was our principal's seat, and already occupied. The dislodged gentleman bounced around for a long breath or two before the Baptist minister gave him his chair, then 33 with more dignity than the situation deserved, the minister walked off the stage.

Donleavy looked at the audience once (on reflection, I'm sure that he wanted only to reassure himself that we were really there), adjusted his glasses, and began to read from a sheaf of papers. 34

He was glad "to be here and to see the work going on just as it was in the other schools." 35

At the first "Amen" from the audience I willed the offender to immediate death by choking on the word. But Amens and Yes, sir's began to fall around the room like rain through a ragged umbrella. 36

He told us of the wonderful changes we children in Stamps had in store. The Central School (naturally, the white school was Central) had already been granted improvements that would be in use in the fall. A well-known artist was coming from Little Rock to teach art to them. They were going to have the newest microscopes and chemistry equipment for their laboratory. Mr. Donleavy didn't leave us long in the dark over who made these improvements available to Central High. Nor were we to be ignored in the general betterment scheme he had in mind. 37

He said that he had pointed out to people at a very high level that one of the first-line football tacklers at Arkansas Agricultural and Mechanical College had graduated from good old Lafayette County Training School. Here fewer Amen's were heard. Those few that did break through lay dully in the air with the heaviness of habit. 38

He went on to praise us. He went on to say how he had bragged that "one of the best basketball players at Fisk sank his first ball right here at Lafayette Training School." 39

The white kids were going to have a chance to become Galileos and Madame Curies and Edisons and Gauguins, and our boys (the girls weren't even in on it) would try to become Jessie Owenses and Joe Louises. 40

Owens and the Brown Bomber were great heroes in our world, but what school official in the white-goddom of Little Rock had the right to decide that those two men must be our only heroes? Who decided that for Henry Reed to become a scientist he had to work like George Washington Carver, as a bootblack, to buy a lousy microscope? Bailey was obviously always going to be too small to be an athlete, so which concrete angel glued to what country seat had decided that if my brother wanted to become a lawyer he had to first pay penance for his skin by picking cotton and hoeing corn and studying correspondence books at night for twenty years? 41

The man's dead words fell like bricks around the auditorium and too many settled in my belly. Constrained by hard-learned manners I couldn't look behind me, but to my left and right the proud graduating class of 1940 had dropped their heads. Every girl in my row had found something to do with her handkerchief. Some folded the tiny 42 squares into love knots, some into triangles, but most were wadding them, then pressing them flat on their yellow laps.

On the dais, the ancient tragedy was being replayed. Professor Parsons sat, a sculptor's reject, rigid. His large, heavy body seemed devoid of will or willingness, and his eyes said he was no longer with us. The other teachers examined the flag (which was draped stage right) or their notes, or the windows which opened on our now-famous playing diamond.   43

Graduation, the hush-hush magic time of frills and gifts and congratulations and diplomas, was finished for me before my name was called. The accomplishment was nothing. The meticulous maps, drawn in three colors of ink, learning and spelling decasyllabic words, memorizing the whole of *The Rape of Lucrece*—it was nothing. Donleavy had exposed us.   44

We were maids and farmers, handymen and washerwomen, and anything higher that we aspired to was farcical and presumptuous. Then I wished that Gabriel Prosser and Nat Turner had killed all the whitefolks in their beds and that Abraham Lincoln had been assassinated before the signing of the Emancipation Proclamation, and that Harriet Tubman had been killed by that blow on her head and Christopher Columbus had drowned in the *Santa Maria*.   45

It was awful to be Negro and have no control over my life. It was brutal to be young and already trained to sit quietly and listen to charges brought against my color with no chance of defense. We should all be dead. I thought I should like to see us all dead, one on top of the other. A pyramid of flesh with the whitefolks at the bottom, as the broad base, then the Indians with their silly tomahawks and teepees and wigwams and treaties, the Negroes with their mops and recipes and cotton sacks and spirituals sticking out of their mouths. The Dutch children should all stumble in their wooden shoes and break their necks. The French should choke to death on the Louisiana Purchase (1803) while silkworms ate all the Chinese with their stupid pigtails. As a species, we were an abomination. All of us.   46

Donleavy was running for election, and assured our parents that if he won we could count on having the only colored playing field in that part of Arkansas. Also—he never looked up to acknowledge the grunts of acceptance—also, we were bound to get new equipment for the home economics building and the workshop.   47

He finished, and since there was no need to give any more than the most perfunctory thank-you's, he nodded to the men on the stage, and the tall white man who was never introduced joined him at the door. They left with the attitude that now they were off to something really important. (The graduation ceremonies at Lafayette County Training School had been a mere preliminary.)   48

The ugliness they left was palpable. An uninvited guest who wouldn't leave. The choir was summoned and sang a modern arrangement of   49

"Onward, Christian Soldiers," with new words pertaining to graduates seeking their place in the world. But it didn't work. Elouise, the daughter of the Baptist minister, recited "Invictus," and I could have cried at the impertinence of "I am the master of my fate, I am the captain of my soul."

My name had lost its ring of familiarity and I had to be nudged to go and receive my diploma. All my preparations had fled. I neither marched up to the stage like a conquering Amazon, nor did I look in the audience for Bailey's nod of approval. Marguerite Johnson, I heard the name again, my honors were read, there were noises in the audience of appreciation, and I took my place on the stage as rehearsed.   50

I thought about colors I hated: ecru, puce, lavender, beige, and black.   51

There was shuffling and rustling around me, then Henry Reed was giving his valedictory address, "To Be or Not to Be." Hadn't he heard the whitefolks? We couldn't *be*, so the question was a waste of time. Henry's voice came out clear and strong. I feared to look at him. Hadn't he got the message: There was no "nobler in the mind" for Negroes because the world didn't think we had minds, and they let us know it. "Outrageous fortune"? Now, that was a joke. When the ceremony was over I had to tell Henry Reed some things. That is, if I still cared. Not "rub," Henry, "erase." "Ah, there's the erase." Us.   52

Henry had been a good student in elocution. His voice rose on tides of promise and fell on waves of warnings. The English teacher had helped him to create a sermon winging through Hamlet's soliloquy. To be a man, a doer, a builder, a leader, or to be a tool, an unfunny joke, a crusher of funky toadstools. I marveled that Henry could go through the speech as if we had a choice.   53

I had been listening and silently rebutting each sentence with my eyes closed; then there was a hush, which in an audience warns that something unplanned is happening. I looked up and saw Henry Reed, the conservative, the proper, the A student, turn his back to the audience and turn to us (the proud graduating class of 1940) and sing, nearly speaking,   54

Lift ev'ry voice and sing
Till earth and heaven ring
Ring with the harmonies of Liberty . . .

It was the poem written by James Weldon Johnson. It was the music composed by J. Rosamond Johnson. It was the Negro National Anthem. Out of habit we were singing it.

Our mothers and fathers stood in the dark hall and joined the hymn of encouragement. A kindergarten teacher led the small children onto the stage and the buttercups and daisies and bunny rabbits marked time and tried to follow: 55

Stony the road we trod
Bitter the chastening rod
Felt in the days when hope, unborn, had died.
Yet with a steady beat
Have not our weary feet
Come to the place for which our fathers sighed?

Every child I knew had learned that song with his ABCs and along   56
with "Jesus Loves Me This I Know." But I personally had never heard it
before. Never heard the words, despite the thousands of times I had
sung them. Never thought they had anything to do with me.

On the other hand, the words of Patrick Henry had made such an   57
impression on me that I had been able to stretch myself tall and trembling and say, "I know not what course others may take, but as for me,
give me liberty or give me death."

And now I heard, really for the first time: 58

We have come over a way that with tears has been watered,
We have come, treading our path through the blood of the
    slaughtered.

While echoes of the song shivered in the air, Henry Reed bowed his   59
head, said "Thank you," and returned to his place in the line. The tears
that slipped down many faces were not wiped away in shame.

We were on top again. As always, again. We survived. The depths   60
had been icy and dark, but now a bright sun spoke to our souls. I was
no longer simply a member of the proud graduating class of 1940; I
was a proud member of the wonderful, beautiful Negro race.

Oh, Black known and unknown poets, how often have your auc-   61
tioned pains sustained us? Who will compute the lonely nights made
less lonely by your songs, or by the empty pots made less tragic by
your tales?

If we were a people much given to revealing secrets, we might raise   62
monuments and sacrifice to the memories of our poets, but slavery
cured us of that weakness. It may be enough, however, to have it said
that we survive in exact relationship to the dedication of our poets
(include preachers, musicians, and blues singers).

QUESTIONS FOR DISCUSSION

1   How does the black community in Stamps feel about the gradua-
    tion and the graduates? What details seem to represent their feel-
    ings? What do they anticipate?

2   Donleavy's expectations for the graduation class of Lafayette
    County Training School undermine the students' spirits. What

images does Angelou develop to convey her sense of disillusion-ment? What lesson has she learned through overcoming her disillusionment?

3 Why does Angleou understand for the first time the spirit behind the Negro National Anthem? In what ways has her community helped her to overcome the humiliation inflicted by Donleavy?

4 Compare and contrast your high school experiences with gender and ethnic discrimination to Maya Angelou's.

5 To what extent have gender and racial attitudes changed in the last fifty years? Refer to specific details and incidents in the selection to support your points.

IDEAS FOR WRITING

1 Write an essay about you graduation from junior high or high school. In what sense was this event a turning point in your life?

2 Do you think that students learn more inside the classroom or through related experiences outside the classroom, such as social and political clubs, peer relationships, or graduation ceremonies? Use specific examples to support your point of view.

Private and Public Language

RICHARD RODRIGUEZ

*Richard Rodriguez became a national figure with the publication
of his memoir,* Hunger of Memory *(1982), in which he opposes bilingual education. Rodriguez, who was born in 1944 to immigrant
parents, grew up in Sacramento and earned his B.A. at Stanford, his
M.A. at Columbia, and his Ph.D. at Berkeley. In* Days of Obligation:
An Argument with My Mexican Father *(1992), Rodriguez expands his
focus to analyze the way Latin American and Asian immigrants are
currently influencing and being transformed by the American experience and culture. As you read "Public and Private Language," which
is excerpted from* Hunger of Memory, *trace Rodriguez's argument
against bilingual education and also consider how his personal
experiences influenced his point of view.*

I remember to start with that day in Sacramento—a California now   1
nearly thirty years past—when I first entered a classroom, able to understand some fifty stray English words.

The third of four children, I had been preceded to a neighborhood   2
Roman Catholic school by an older brother and sister. But neither of
them had revealed very much about their classroom experiences. Each
afternoon they returned, as they left in the morning, always together,
speaking Spanish as they climbed the five steps of the porch. And their
mysterious books, wrapped in shopping-bag paper, remained on the
table next to the door, closed firmly behind them.

An accident of geography sent me to a school where all my class-   3
mates were white, many the children of doctors and lawyers and business executives. All my classmates certainly must have been uneasy
on that first day of school—as most children are uneasy—to find
themselves apart from their families in the first institution of their
lives. But I was astonished.

The nun said, in a friendly but oddly impersonal voice, "Boys and   4
girls, this is Richard Rodriguez." (I heard her sound out: *Rich-heard
Road-ree-guess.*) It was the first time I had heard anyone name me in
English. "Richard," the nun repeated more slowly, writing my name
down in her black leather book. Quickly I turned to see my mother's
face dissolve in a watery blur behind the pebbled glass door.

Many years later there is something called bilingual education—a   5
scheme proposed in the late 1960s by Hispanic-American social ac-
tivists, later endorsed by a congressional vote. It was a program that
seeks to permit non-English-speaking children, many from lower-
class homes, to use their family language as the language of school.

(Such is the goal its supporters announce.) I hear them and am forced to say no: It is not possible for a child—any child—ever to use his family's language in school. Not to understand this is to misunderstand the public uses of schooling and to trivialize the nature of intimate life—a family's "language."

Memory teaches me what I know of these matters; the boy reminds   6
the adult. I was a bilingual child, a certain kind—socially disadvantaged—the son of working-class parents, both Mexican immigrants.

In the early years of my boyhood, my parents coped very well in   7
America. My father had steady work. My mother managed at home. They were nobody's victims. Optimism and ambition led them to a house (our home) many blocks from the Mexican south side of town. We lived among *gringos* and only a block from the biggest, whitest houses. It never occurred to my parents that they couldn't live wherever they chose. Nor was the Sacramento of the fifties bent on teaching them a contrary lesson. My mother and father were more annoyed than intimidated by those two or three neighbors who tried initially to make us unwelcome. ("Keep your brats away from my sidewalk!") but despite all they achieved, perhaps because they had so much to achieve, any deep feeling of ease, the confidence of "belonging" in public was withheld from them both. They regarded the people at work, the faces in crowds, as very distant from us. They were the others, *los gringos*. That term was interchangeable in their speech with another, even more telling, *los americanos*.

I grew up in a house where the only regular guests were my rela-   8
tions. For one day, enormous families of relatives would visit and there would be so many people that the noise and the bodies would spill out to the backyard and front porch. Then, for weeks, no one came by. (It was usually a salesman who rang the doorbell.) Our house stood apart. A gaudy yellow in a row of white bungalows. We were the people with the noisy dog. The people who raised pigeons and chickens. We were the foreigners on the block. A few neighbors smiled and waved. We waved back. But no one in the family knew the names of the old couple who lived next door; until I was seven years old, I did not know the names of the kids who lived across the street.

In public, my father and mother spoke a hesitant, accented, not   9
always grammatical English. And they would have to strain—their bodies tense—to catch the sense of what was rapidly being said by *los gringos*. At home they spoke Spanish. The language of their Mexican past sounded in counterpoint to the English of public society. The words would come quickly, with ease. Conveyed through those sounds was the pleasing, soothing, consoling reminder of being at home.

During those years when I was first conscious of hearing, my   10
mother and father addressed me only in Spanish; in Spanish I learned to reply. By contrast, English (*inglés*), rarely heard in the house, was the language I came to associate with *gringos*. I learned my first words

of English overhearing my parents speak to strangers. At five years of age, I knew just enough English for my mother to trust me on errands to stores one block away. No more.

I was a listening child, careful to hear the very different sounds of Spanish and English. Wide-eyed with hearing, I'd listen to sounds more than words. First, there were English (*gringo*) sounds. So many words were still unknown that when the butcher or the lady at the drugstore said something to me, exotic polysyllabic sounds would bloom in the midst of their sentences. Often, the speech of people in public seemed to me very loud, booming with confidence. The man behind the counter would literally ask, "What can I do for you?" But by being firm and so clear, the sound of his voice said that he was a *gringo*; he belonged in public society. [11]

I would also hear then the high nasal notes of middle-class American speech. The air stirred with sounds. Sometimes, even now, when I have been traveling abroad for several weeks, I will hear what I heard as a boy. In hotel lobbies or airports, in Turkey or Brazil, some Americans will pass, and suddenly I will hear it again—the high sound of American voices. For a few seconds I will hear it with pleasure, for it is now the sound of *my* society—a reminder of home. But inevitably— already on the flight headed for home—the sound fades with repetition. I will be unable to hear it anymore. [12]

When I was a boy, things were different. The accent of *los gringos* was never pleasing nor was it hard to hear. Crowds at Safeway or at bus stops would be noisy with sound. And I would be forced to edge away from the chirping chatter above me. [13]

I was unable to hear my own sounds, but I knew very well that I spoke English poorly. My words could not stretch far enough to form complete thoughts. And the words I did speak I didn't know well enough to make into distinct sounds. (Listeners would usually lower their heads, better to hear what I was trying to say.) But it was one thing for *me* to speak English with difficulty. It was more troubling for me to hear my parents speak in public: their high-whining vowels and guttural consonants; their sentences that got stuck with "eh" and "ah" sounds; the confused syntax; the hesitant rhythm of sounds so different from the way *gringos* spoke. I'd notice, moreover, that my parents' voices were softer than those of *gringos* we'd meet. [14]

I am tempted now to say that none of this mattered. In adulthood I am embarrassed by childhood fears. And, in a way, it didn't matter very much that my parents could not speak English with ease. Their linguistic difficulties had no serious consequences. My mother and father made themselves understood at the county hospital clinic and at government offices. And yet, in another way, it mattered very much—it was unsettling to hear my parents struggle with English. Hearing them, I'd grow nervous, my clutching trust in their protection and power weakened. [15]

There were many times like the night at a brightly lit gasoline station   16
(a blaring white memory) when I stood uneasily, hearing my father. He
was talking to a teenaged attendant. I do not recall what they were saying, but I cannot forget the sounds my father made as he spoke. At one
point his words slid together to form one word—sounds as confused
as the threads of blue and green oil in the puddle next to my shoes. His
voice rushed through what he had left to say. And, toward the end,
reached falsetto notes, appealing to his listener's understanding. I
looked away to the lights of passing automobiles. I tried not to hear
anymore. But I heard only too well the calm, easy tones in the attendant's reply. Shortly afterward, walking toward home with my father, I
shivered when he put his hand on my shoulder. The very first chance
that I got, I evaded his grasp and ran on ahead into the dark, skipping
with feigned boyish exuberance.

But then there was Spanish. *Español*: my family's language. *Español*:   17
the language that seemed to me a private language. I'd hear strangers
on the radio and in the Mexican Catholic church across town speaking
Spanish, but I couldn't really believe that Spanish was a public language, like English. Spanish speakers, rather, seemed related to me, for
I sensed that we shared—through our language—the experience of
feeling apart from *los gringos*. It was thus a ghetto Spanish that I heard
and I spoke. Like those whose lives are bound by a barrio, I was reminded by Spanish of my separateness from *los otros, los gringos* in
power. But more intensely than for most barrio children—because I
did not live in a barrio—Spanish seemed to me the language of home.
(Most days it was only at home that I'd hear it.) It became the language
of joyful return.

A family member would say something to me and I would feel my-   18
self specially recognized. My parents would say something to me and
I would feel embraced by the sounds of their words. Those sounds
said: *I am speaking with ease in Spanish. I am addressing you in words
I never use with* los gringos. *I recognize you as someone special, close,
like no one outside. You belong to us. In the family.*

(*Ricardo.*)   19

At the age of five, six, well past the time when most other children   20
no longer easily notice the difference between sounds uttered at
home and words spoken in public, I had a different experience. I lived
in a world magically compounded of sounds. I remained a child
longer than most; I lingered too long, poised at the edge of language—
often frightened by the sounds of *los gringos*, delighted by the sounds
of Spanish at home. I shared with my family a language that was
startlingly different from that used in the great city around us.

For me there was none of the gradations between public and pri-   21
vate society so normal to a maturing child. Outside the house was
public society; inside the house was private. Just opening or closing
the screen door behind me was an important experience. I'd rarely

leave home all alone or without reluctance. Walking down the side-walk, under the canopy of tall trees, I'd warily notice the—suddenly—silent neighborhood kids who stood warily watching me. Nervously, I'd arrive at the grocery store to hear there the sounds of the *gringo*—foreign to me—reminding me that in this world so big, I was a for-eigner. But then I'd return. Walking back toward our house, climbing the steps from the sidewalk, when the front door was open in sum-mer, I'd hear voices beyond the screen door talking in Spanish. For a second or two, I'd stay, linger there, listening. Smiling, I'd hear my mother call out, saying in Spanish (words): "Is that you, Richard?" All the while her sounds would assure me: *You are home now; come closer; inside. With us.*

"*Sí*," I'd reply.   22

Once more inside the house I would resume (assume) my place in   23
the family. The sounds would dim, grow harder to hear. Once more at home, I would grow less aware of that fact. It required, however, no more than the blurt of the doorbell to alert me to listen to sounds all over again. The house would turn instantly still while my mother went to the door. I'd hear her hard English sounds. I'd wait to hear her voice return to soft-sounding Spanish, which assured me, as surely as did the clicking tongue of the lock on the door, that the stranger was gone.

Plainly, it is not healthy to hear such sounds so often. It is not   24
healthy to distinguish public words from private sounds so easily. I re-mained cloistered by sounds, timid and shy in public, too dependent on voices at home. And yet it needs to be emphasized: I was an ex-tremely happy child at home. I remember many nights when my father would come back from work, and I'd hear him call out to my mother in Spanish, sounding relieved. In Spanish, he'd sound light and free notes he never could manage in English. Some nights I'd jump up just at hearing his voice. With *mis hermanos* I would come running into the room where he was with my mother. Our laughing (so deep was the pleasure!) became screaming. Like others who know the pain of pub-lic alienation, we transformed the knowledge of our public separate-ness and made it consoling—the reminder of intimacy. *We are speaking now the way we never speak out in public. We are alone—together*, voices sounded, surrounded to tell me. Some nights, no one seemed willing to loosen the hold sounds had on us. At dinner, we invented new words. (Ours sounded Spanish, but made sense only to us.) We pieced together new words by taking, say, an English verb and giving it Spanish endings. My mother's instructions at bedtime would be lacquered with mock-urgent tones. Or a word like *sí* would be-come, in several notes, able to convey added measures of feeling. Tongues explored the edges of words, especially the fat vowels. And we happily sounded that military drum roll, the twirling roar of the Spanish *r*. Family language: my family's sounds. The voices of my parents and sisters and brother. Their voices insisting: *You belong*

here. We are family members. Related. Special to one another. Listen!
Voices singing and sighing, rising, straining, then surging, teeming
with pleasure that burst syllables into fragments of laughter. At times
it seemed there was steady quiet only when, from another room, the
rustling whispers of my parents faded and I moved closer to sleep.

Supporters of bilingual education today imply that students like   25
me miss a great deal by not being taught in their family's language.
What they seem not to recognize is that, as a socially disadvantaged
child, I considered Spanish to be a private language. What I needed to
learn in school was that I had the right—and the obligation—to speak
the public language of *los gringos*. The odd truth is that my first-grade
classmates could have become bilingual, in the conventional sense of
that word, more easily than I. Had they been taught (as upper-middle-
class children are often taught early) a second language like Spanish or
French, they could have regarded it simply as that: another public
language. In my case such bilingualism could not have been so quickly
achieved. What I did not believe was that I could speak a single public language.

Without question, it would have pleased me to hear my teachers   26
address me in Spanish when I entered the classroom. I would have felt
much less afraid. I would have trusted them and responded with ease.
But I would have delayed—for how long postponed?—having to learn
the language of public society. I would have evaded—and for how
long could I have afforded to delay?—learning the great lesson of
school, that I had a public identity.

Fortunately, my teachers were unsentimental about their responsi-   27
bility. What they understood was that I needed to speak a public language. So their voices would search me out, asking me questions.
Each time I'd hear them, I'd look up in surprise to see a nun's face
frowning at me. I'd mumble, not really meaning to answer. The nun
would persist, "Richard, stand up. Don't look at the floor. Speak up.
Speak to the entire class, not just to me!" But I couldn't believe that the
English language was mine to use. (In part, I did not want to believe
it.) I continued to mumble. I resisted the teacher's demands. (Did I
somehow suspect that once I learned public language my pleasing
family life would be changed?) Silent, waiting for the bell to sound, I
remained dazed, diffident, afraid.

Because I wrongly imagined that English was intrinsically a public   28
language and Spanish an intrinsically private one, I easily noted the
difference between the classroom language and the language of home.
At school, words were directed to a general audience of listeners.
("Boys and girls.") Words were meaningfully ordered. And the point
was not self-expression alone but to make oneself understood by
many others. The teacher quizzed: "Boys and girls, why do we use that
word in this sentence? Could we think of a better word to use there?

Would the sentence change its meaning if the words were differently arranged? And wasn't there a better way of saying much the same thing?" (I couldn't say. I wouldn't try to say.)

Three months. Five. Half a year passed. Unsmiling, ever watchful, my teachers noted my silence. They began to connect my behavior with the difficult progress my older sister and brother were making. Until one Saturday morning three nuns arrived at the house to talk to our parents. Stiffly, they sat on the blue living room sofa. From the doorway of another room, spying the visitors, I noted the incongruity—the clash of two worlds, the faces and voices of school intruding upon the familiar setting of home. I overheard one voice gently wondering, "Do your children speak only Spanish at home, Mrs. Rodriguez?" While another voice added, "That Richard especially seems so timid and shy."   29

That Rich-heard!   30

With great tact the visitors continued, "Is it possible for you and your husband to encourage your children to practice their English when they are home?" Of course, my parents complied. What would they not do for their children's well-being? And how could they have questioned the Church's authority which those women represented? In an instant, they agreed to give up the language (the sounds) that had revealed and accentuated our family's closeness. The moment after the visitors left, the change was observed. "*Ahora*, speak to us *en inglés*," my father and mother united to tell us.   31

At first, it seemed a kind of game. After dinner each night, the family gathered to practice "our" English. (It was still then *inglés*, a language foreign to us, so we felt drawn as strangers to it.) Laughing, we would try to define words we could not pronounce. We played with strange English sounds, often over-anglicizing our pronunciations. And we filled the smiling gaps of our sentences with familiar Spanish sounds. But that was cheating, somebody shouted. Everyone laughed. In school, meanwhile, like my brother and sister, I was required to attend a daily tutoring session. I needed a full year of special attention. I also needed my teachers to keep my attention from straying in class by calling out, *Rich-heard*—their English voices slowly prying loose my ties to my other name, its three notes, *Ri-car-do*. Most of all I needed to hear my mother and father speak to me in a moment of seriousness in broken—suddenly heartbreaking—English. The scene was inevitable: One Saturday morning I entered the kitchen where my parents were talking in Spanish. I did not realize that they were talking in Spanish however until, at the moment they saw me, I heard their voices change to speak English. Those *gringo* sounds they uttered startled me. Pushed me away. In that moment of trivial misunderstanding and profound insight, I felt my throat twisted by unsounded grief. I turned quickly and left the room. But I had no place to escape to with Spanish. (The spell was broken.) My brother and sisters were speaking English in another part of the house.   32

Again and again in the days following, increasingly angry, I was   33
obliged to hear my mother and father: "Speak to us *en inglés.*" (*Speak.*)
Only then did I determine to learn classroom English. Weeks after, it
happened: One day in school I raised my hand to volunteer an answer.
I spoke out in a loud voice. And I did not think it remarkable when the
entire class understood. That day, I moved very far from the disadvantaged child I had been only days earlier. The belief, the calming assurance that I belonged in public, had at last taken hold.

Shortly after, I stopped hearing the high and loud sounds of *los*   34
gringos. A more and more confident speaker of English, I didn't trouble
to listen to *how* strangers sounded, speaking to me. And there simply
were too many English-speaking people in my day for me to hear
American accents anymore. Conversations quickened. Listening to
persons who sounded eccentrically pitched voices, I usually noted
their sounds for an initial few seconds before I concentrated on *what*
they were saying. Conversations became content-full. Transparent.
Hearing someone's *tone* of voice—angry or questioning or sarcastic or
happy or sad—I didn't distinguish it from the words it expressed.
Sound and word were thus tightly wedded. At the end of the day, I was
often bemused, always relieved, to realize how "silent," though
crowded with words, my day in public had been. (This public silence
measured and quickened the change in my life.)

At last, seven years old, I came to believe what had been technically   35
true since my birth: I was an American citizen.

But the special feeling of closeness at home was diminished by   36
then. Gone was the desperate, urgent, intense feeling of being at
home; rare was the experience of feeling myself individualized by
family intimates. We remained a loving family, but one greatly
changed. No longer so close; no longer bound tight by the pleasing
and troubling knowledge of public separateness. Neither my older
brother nor sister rushed home after school anymore. Nor did I. When
I arrived home there would often be neighborhood kids in the house.
Or the house would be empty of sounds.

Following the dramatic Americanization of their children, even my   37
parents grew more publicly confident. Especially my mother. She
learned the names of all the people on our block. And she decided we
needed to have a telephone installed in the house. My father continued to use the word *gringo*. But it was no longer charged with the
old bitterness or distrust. (Stripped of any emotional content, the word
simply became a name for those Americans not of Hispanic descent.)
Hearing him, sometimes, I wasn't sure if he was pronouncing the
Spanish word *gringo* or saying gringo in English.

Matching the silence I started hearing in public was a new quiet at   38
home. The family's quiet was partly due to the fact that, as we children
learned more and more English, we shared fewer and fewer words
with our parents. Sentences needed to be spoken slowly when a child

addressed his mother or father. (Often the parent wouldn't understand.) The child would need to repeat himself. (Still the parent misunderstood.) The young voice, frustrated, would end up saying, "Never mind"—the subject was closed. Dinners would be noisy with the clinking of knives and forks against dishes. My mother would smile softly between her remarks; my father at the other end of the table would chew and chew at his food, while he stared over the heads of his children.

My *mother!* My *father!* After English became my primary language, I 39
no longer knew what words to use in addressing my parents. The old Spanish words (those tender accents of sounds) I had used earlier— *mamá* and *papá*—I couldn't use anymore. They would have been too painful reminders of how much had changed in my life. On the other hand, the words I heard neighborhood kids call *their* parents seemed equally unsatisfactory. *Mother* and *Father; Ma, Papa, Pa, Dad, Pop* (how I hated the all-American sound of that last word especially)—all these terms I felt were unsuitable, not really terms of address for *my* parents. As I result, I never used them at home. Whenever I'd speak to my parents, I would try to get their attention with eye contact alone. In public conversations, I'd refer to "my parents" or "my mother and father."

My mother and father, for their part, responded differently, as their 40
children spoke to them less. She grew restless, seemed troubled and anxious at the scarcity of words exchanged in the house. It was she who would question me about my day when I came home from school. She smiled at small talk. She pried at the edges of my sentences to get me to say something more. (What?) She'd join conversations she overheard, but her intrusions often stopped her children's talking. By contrast, my father seemed reconciled to the new quiet. Though his English improved somewhat, he retired into silence. At dinner he spoke very little. One night his children and even his wife helplessly giggled at his garbled English pronunciation of the Catholic Grace before Meals. Thereafter he made his wife recite the prayer at the start of each meal, even on formal occasions, when there were guests in the house. Hers became the public voice of the family. On official business, it was she, not my father, one would usually hear on the phone or in stores, talking to strangers. His children grew so accustomed to his silence that, years later, they would speak routinely of his shyness. (My mother would often try to explain: Both his parents died when he was eight. He was raised by an uncle who treated him like little more than a menial servant. He was never encouraged to speak. He grew up alone. A man of few words.) But my father was not shy, I realized, when I'd watch him speaking Spanish with relatives. Using Spanish, he was quickly effusive. Especially when talking with other men, his voice would spark, flicker, flare alive with sounds. In Spanish, he expressed ideas and feelings he rarely revealed in English. With firm Spanish sounds, he conveyed confidence and authority English would never allow him.

The silence at home, however was finally more than a literal silence. 41
Fewer words passed between parent and child, but more profound was
the silence that resulted from my inattention to sounds. At about the
time I no longer bothered to listen with care to the sounds of English in
public, I grew careless about listening to the sounds family members
made when they spoke. Most of the time I heard someone speaking at
home and didn't distinguish his sound from the words people uttered
in public. I didn't even pay much attention to my parents' accented and
ungrammatical speech. At least not at home. Only when I was with
them in public would I grow alert to their accents. Though, even then,
their sounds caused me less and less concern. For I was increasingly
confident in my own public identity.

I would have been happier about my public success had I not 42
sometimes recalled what it had been like earlier, when my family had
conveyed its intimacy through a set of conveniently private sounds.
Sometimes in public, hearing a stranger, I'd hark back to my past. A
Mexican farmworker approached me downtown to ask directions to
somewhere. "*¿Hijito . . . ?*" he said. And his voice summoned deep
longing. Another time, standing beside my mother in the visiting
room of a Carmelite convent, before the dense screen which ren-
dered the nuns shadowy figures, I heard several Spanish-speaking
nuns—their busy, singsong overlapping voices—assure us that yes,
yes, we were remembered, all our family was remembered in their
prayers. (Their voices echoed faraway family sounds.) Another day, a
dark-faced old woman—her hand light on my shoulder—steadied
herself against me as she boarded a bus. She murmured something I
couldn't quite comprehend. Her Spanish voice came near, like the
face of a never-before-seen relative in the instant before I was kissed.
Her voice, like so many of the Spanish voices I'd hear in public, recalled the golden age of my youth. Hearing Spanish then, I continued
to be a careful, if sad, listener to sounds. Hearing a Spanish-speaking
family walking behind me, I turned to look. I smiled for an instant,
before my glance found the Hispanic-looking faces of strangers in
the crowd going by.

Today I hear bilingual educators say that children lose a degree of 43
"individuality" by becoming assimilated into public society. (Bilingual
schooling was popularized in the seventies, that decade when middle-
class ethnics began to resist the process of assimilation—the American
melting pot.) But the bilingualists simplistically scorn the value and
necessity of assimilation. They do not seem to realize that there are
two ways a person is individualized. So they do not realize that while
one suffers a diminished sense of *private* individuality by becoming
assimilated into public society, such assimilation makes possible the
achievement of *public* individuality.

The bilingualists insist that a student should be reminded of his difference from others in mass society, his heritage. But they equate mere separateness with individuality. The fact is that only in private—with intimates—is separateness from the crowd a prerequisite for individuality. (An intimate draws me apart, tells me that I am unique, unlike all others.) In public, by contrast, full individuality is achieved, paradoxically, by those who are able to consider themselves members of the crowd. Thus it happened for me: Only when I was able to think of myself as an American, no longer an alien in *gringo* society, could I seek the rights and opportunities necessary for full public individuality. The social and political advantages I enjoy as a man result from the day that I came to believe that my name, indeed, is *Rich-heard Road-ree-guess*. It is true that my public society is often impersonal. (My public society is usually mass society.) Yet despite the anonymity of the crowd and despite the fact that the individuality I achieve in public is often tenuous—because it depends on my being one in a crowd—I celebrate the day I acquired my new name. Those middle-class ethnics who scorn assimilation seem to me filled with decadent self-pity, obsessed by the burden of public life. Dangerously, they romanticize public separateness and they trivialize the dilemma of the socially disadvantaged.

My awkward childhood does not prove the necessity of bilingual education. My story discloses instead an essential myth of childhood—inevitable pain. If I rehearse here the changes in my private life after my Americanization, it is finally to emphasize the public gain. The loss implies the gain: The house I returned to each afternoon was quiet. Intimate sounds no longer rushed to greet me. There were other noises inside. The telephone rang. Neighborhood kids ran past the door of the bedroom where I was reading my schoolbooks—covered with shopping-bag paper. Once I learned public language, it would never again be easy for me to hear intimate family voices. More and more of my day was spent hearing words. But that may only be a way of saying that the day I raised my hand in class and spoke loudly to an entire roomful of faces, my childhood started to end.

QUESTIONS FOR DISCUSSION

1 Discuss your family's use of English when you were growing up. How did their values and assumptions about the correct and comfortable ways to use language help to shape the way you use language? Do you have a sense of private and public language as Rodriguez does?

2 Why does Rodriguez think that bilingual education would not have helped him to succeed in learning English? What finally motivates him to speak English at school?

3   Contrast Rodriguez's home life to his school life when he was growing up. Why does the family's acceptance of English create a growing silence at their home?

4   Why does Rodriguez distinguish between Spanish and English (*gringo*) sounds? How does he deepen the meaning and importance of language through his comparison?

5   Rodriguez's essay was written about his experiences growing up in the 1950s. Would Rodriguez's experience have been different if he were attending school in the late 1990s?

IDEAS FOR WRITING

1   Rodriguez believes, "It is not possible for a child, any child, ever to use his family's language in school. Not to understand this is to misunderstand the public uses of schooling and to trivialize the nature of intimate life." Write an argument that supports or refutes Rodriguez's position.

2   Develop a proposal for improving the quality of education for minority students at your local high school. Include concrete reasons based on your experiences in high school classes to support your proposal.

Keeping Close to Home: Class and Education

BELL HOOKS

Hooks is one of America's best-known black intellectuals. Currently she teaches English and African American literature at Oberlin College in Ohio. Born Gloria Watkins in rural Kentucky in 1952, hooks earned her master's degree from the University of Wisconsin–Madison and her Ph.D. at Stanford University. Among her best-known books are the autobiographical Ain't I a Woman *(1981) and the essay collections* Talking Back, Thinking Feminist, Thinking Black *(1989),* Black Looks: Race and Representation *(1992), and* Killing Rage *(1995). Most recently she has published* Bone Black: Memories of Girlhood *(1996) and* Reel to Real: Race, Sex and Class at the Movies *(1997). In her writing about cultural, gender, and ethnic issues, hooks always reflects deeply upon her own experiences. In the following selection from* Talking Back, *she writes about her struggle to be educated.*

We are both awake in the almost dark of 5 A.M. Everyone else is   1
sound asleep. Mama asks the usual questions. Telling me to look around, make sure I have everything, scolding because I am uncertain about the actual time the bus arrives. By 5:30 we are waiting outside the closed station. Alone together, we have a chance to really talk. Mama begins. Angry with her children, especially the ones who whisper behind her back, she says bitterly, "Your childhood could not have been that bad. You were fed and clothed. You did not have to do without—that's more than a lot of folks have and I just can't stand the way y'all go on." The hurt in her voice saddens me. I have always wanted to protect mama from hurt, to ease her burdens. Now I am part of what troubles. Confronting me, she says accusingly, "It's not just the other children. You talk too much about the past. You don't just listen." And I do talk. Worse, I write about it.

Mama has always come to each of her children seeking different   2
responses. With me she expresses the disappointment, hurt, and anger of betrayal: anger that her children are so critical, that we can't even have the sense to like the presents she sends. She says, "From now on there will be no presents. I'll just stick some money in a little envelope the way the rest of you do. Nobody wants criticism. Everybody can criticize me but I am supposed to say nothing." When I try to talk, my voice sounds like a twelve year old. When I try to talk, she speaks louder, interrupting me, even though she has said repeatedly, "Explain it to me, this talk about the past." I struggle to return to my thirty-five year old self so that she will know by the sound of my voice that we are two women talking together. It is only when I state firmly

in my very adult voice, "Mama, you are not listening," that she becomes quiet. She waits. Now that I have her attention, I fear that my explanations will be lame, inadequate. "Mama," I begin, "people usually go to therapy because they feel hurt inside, because they have pain that will not stop, like a wound that continually breaks open, that does not heal. And often these hurts, that pain has to do with things that have happened in the past, sometimes in childhood, often in childhood, or things that we believe happened." She wants to know, "What hurts, what hurts are you talking about?" "Mom, I can't answer that. I can't speak for all of us, the hurts are different for everybody. But the point is you try to make the hurt better, to heal it, by understanding how it came to be. And I know you feel mad when we say something happened or hurt that you don't remember being that way, but the past isn't like that, we don't have the same memory of it. We remember things differently. You know that. And sometimes folk feel hurt about stuff and you just don't know or didn't realize it, and they need to talk about it. Surely you understand the need to talk about it."

Our conversation is interrupted by the sight of my uncle walking 3
across the park toward us. We stop to watch him. He is on his way to work dressed in a familiar blue suit. They look alike, these two who rarely discuss the past. This interruption makes me think about life in a small town. You always see someone you know. Interruptions, intrusions are part of daily life. Privacy is difficult to maintain. We leave our private space in the car to greet him. After the hug and kiss he has given me every year since I was born, they talk about the day's funerals. In the distance the bus approaches. He walks away knowing that they will see each other later. Just before I board the bus I turn, staring into my mother's face. I am momentarily back in time, seeing myself eighteen years ago, at this same bus stop, staring into my mother's face, continually turning back, waving farewell as I returned to college—that experience which first took me away from our town, from family. Departing was as painful then as it is now. Each movement away makes return harder. Each separation intensifies distance, both physical and emotional.

To a southern black girl from a working-class background who had 4
never been on a city bus, who had never stepped on an escalator, who had never travelled by plane, leaving the comfortable confines of a small town Kentucky life to attend Stanford University was not just frightening; it was utterly painful. My parents had not been delighted that I had been accepted and adamantly opposed my going so far from home. At the time, I did not see their opposition as an expression of their fear that they would lose me forever. Like many working-class folks, they feared what college education might do to their children's minds even as they unenthusiastically acknowledged its importance. They did not understand why I could not attend a college nearby, an all-black college. To them, any college would do. I would graduate,

become a school teacher, make a decent living and good marriage. And even though they reluctantly and skeptically supported my educational endeavors, they also subjected them to constant harsh and bitter critique. It is difficult for me to talk about my parents and their impact on me because they have always felt wary, ambivalent, mistrusting of my intellectual aspirations even as they have been caring and supportive. I want to speak about these contradictions because sorting through them, seeking resolution and reconciliation has been important to me both as it affects my development as a writer, my effort to be fully self-realized, and my longing to remain close to the family and community that provided the groundwork for much of my thinking, writing, and being.

Studying at Stanford, I began to think seriously about class differ- 5 ences. To be materially underprivileged at a university where most folks (with the exceptions of workers) are materially privileged provokes such thought. Class differences were boundaries no one wanted to face or talk about. It was easier to downplay them, to act as though we were all from privileged backgrounds, to work around them, to confront them privately in the solitude of one's room, or to pretend that just being chosen to study at such an institution meant that those of us who did not come from privilege were already in transition toward privilege. To not long for such transition marked one as rebellious, as unlikely to succeed. It was a kind of treason not to believe that it was better to be identified with the world of material privilege than with the world of the working class, the poor. No wonder our working-class parents from poor backgrounds feared our entry into such a world, intuiting perhaps that we might learn to be ashamed of where we had come from, that we might never return home, or come back only to lord it over them.

Though I hung with students who were supposedly radical and 6 chic, we did not discuss class. I talked to no one about the sources of my shame, how it hurt me to witness the contempt shown the brown-skinned Filipina maids who cleaned our rooms, or later my concern about the $100 a month I paid for a room off-campus which was more than half of what my parents paid for rent. I talked to no one about my efforts to save money, to send a little something home. Yet these class realities separated me from fellow students. We were moving in different directions. I did not intend to forget my class background or alter my class allegiance. And even though I received an education designed to provide me with a bourgeois sensibility, passive acquiescence was not my only option. I knew that I could resist. I could rebel. I could shape the direction and focus of the various forms of knowledge available to me. Even though I sometimes envied and longed for greater material advantages (particularly at vacation times when I would be one of few if any students remaining in the dormitory because there was no money for travel), I did not share the sensibility and values of my peers. That was important—class was not just about money; it was about values which showed and determined behavior. While I often needed more money, I never needed a new set of beliefs and values. For example, I was profoundly shocked and disturbed when my peers would talk about their parents without respect, or would even say that they hated their parents. This was especially troubling to me when it seemed that these parents were caring and concerned. It was often explained to me that such hatred was "healthy and normal." To my white, middle-class California roommate, I explained the way we were taught to value our parents and their care, to understand that they were obligated to give us care. She would always shake her head, laughing all the while, and say, "Missy, you will learn that it's different here, that we think differently." She was right. Soon, I lived alone, like the one Mormon student who kept to himself as he made a concentrated effort to remain true to his religious beliefs and values. Later in graduate school I found that classmates believed "lower class" people had no beliefs and values. I was silent in such discussions, disgusted by their ignorance.

Carol Stack's anthropological study, *All Our Kin*, was one of the first books I read which confirmed my experiential understanding that within black culture (especially among the working class and poor, particularly in southern states), a value system emerged that was counter-hegemonic, that challenged notions of individualism and private property so important to the maintenance of white-supremacist, capitalist patriarchy. Black folk created in marginal spaces a world of community and collectivity where resources were shared. In the preface to *Feminist Theory: from margin to center*, I talked about how the point of difference, this marginality, can be the space for the formulation of an oppositional world view. That world view must be articulated, named if it is to provide a sustained blueprint for change. Unfortunately, there has existed no consistent framework for such naming. Consequently both the experience of this difference and documentation of it (when it occurs) gradually loses presence and meaning.

Much of what Stack documented about the "culture of poverty," for example, would not describe interactions among most black poor today irrespective of geographical setting. Since the black people she described did not acknowledge (if they recognized it in theoretical terms) the oppositional value of their world view, apparently seeing it more as a survival strategy determined less by conscious efforts to oppose oppressive race and class biases than by circumstance, they did not attempt to establish a framework to transmit their beliefs and values from generation to generation. When circumstances changed, values altered. Efforts to assimilate the values and beliefs of privileged white people, presented through media like television, undermine and destroy potential structures of opposition.

Increasingly, young black people are encouraged by the dominant   9
culture (and by those black people who internalize the values of this
hegemony) to believe that assimilation is the only way to survive, to
succeed. Without the framework of an organized civil rights or black
resistance struggle, individual and collective efforts at black liberation
that focus on the primacy of self-definition and self-determination
often go unrecognized. It is crucial that those among us who resist
and rebel, who survive and succeed, speak openly and honestly
about our lives and the nature of our personal struggles, the means
by which we resolve and reconcile contradictions. This is no easy
task. Within the educational institutions where we learn to develop
and strengthen our writing and analytical skills, we also learn to think,
write, and talk in a manner that shifts attention away from personal
experience. Yet if we are to reach our people and all people, if we are
to remain connected (especially those of us whose familial backgrounds are poor and working-class), we must understand that the
telling of one's personal story provides a meaningful example, a way
for folks to identify and connect.

Combining personal with critical analysis and theoretical perspec-   10
tives can engage listeners who might otherwise feel estranged, alienated. To speak simply with language that is accessible to as many folks
as possible is also important. Speaking about one's personal experience
or speaking with simple language is often considered by academics
and/or intellectuals (irrespective of their political inclinations) to be a
sign of intellectual weakness or even anti-intellectualism. Lately, when
I speak, I do not stand in place—reading my paper, making little or
no eye contact with audiences—but instead make eye contact, talk ex-
temporaneously, digress, and address the audience directly. I have been
told that people assume I am not prepared, that I am anti-intellectual,
unprofessional (a concept that has everything to do with class as it
determines actions and behaviors), or that I am reinforcing the stereotype of black as non-theoretical and gutsy.

Such criticism was raised recently by fellow feminist scholars after   11
a talk I gave at Northwestern University at a conference on "Gender,
Culture, Politics" to an audience that was mainly students and academics. I deliberately chose to speak in a very basic way, thinking
especially about the few community folks that had come to hear me.
Weeks later, KumKum Sangari, a fellow participant who shared with
me what was said when I was no longer present, and I engaged in
quite rigorous critical dialogue about the way my presentation had
been perceived primarily by privileged white female academics. She
was concerned that I not mask my knowledge of theory, that I not
appear anti-intellectual. Her critique compelled me to articulate concerns that I am often silent about with colleagues. I spoke about class
allegiance and revolutionary commitments, explaining that it was disturbing to me that intellectual radicals who speak about transforming

society, ending the domination of race, sex, class, cannot break with behavior patterns that reinforce and perpetuate domination, or continue to use as their sole reference point how we might be or are perceived by those who dominate, whether or not we gain their acceptance and approval.

This is a primary contradiction which raises the issue of whether or not the academic setting is a place where one can be truly radical or subversive. Concurrently, the use of language and style of presentation that alienates most folks who are not academically trained reinforces the notion that the academic world is separate from real life, that everyday world where we constantly adjust our language and behavior to meet diverse needs. The academic setting is separate only when we work to make it so. It is a false dichotomy which suggests that academics and/or intellectuals can only speak to one another, that we cannot hope to speak with the masses. What is true is that we make choices, that we choose our audiences, that we choose voices to hear and voices to silence. If I do not speak in a language that can be understood, then there is little chance for dialogue. This issue of language and behavior is a central contradiction all radical intellectuals, particularly those who are members of oppressed groups, must continually confront and work to resolve. One of the clear and present dangers that exists when we move outside our class of origin, our collective ethnic experience, and enter hierarchical institutions which daily reinforce domination by race, sex, and class, is that we gradually assume a mindset similar to those who dominate and oppress, that we lose critical consciousness because it is not reinforced or affirmed by the environment. We must be ever vigilant. It is important that we know who we are speaking to, who we most want to hear us, who we most long to move, motivate, and touch with our words.

When I first came to New Haven to teach at Yale, I was truly surprised by the marked class divisions between black folks—students and professors—who identify with Yale and those black folks who work at Yale or in surrounding communities. Style of dress and self-presentation are most often the central markers of one's position. I soon learned that the black folks who spoke on the street were likely to be part of the black community and those who carefully shifted their glance were likely to be associated with Yale. Walking with a black female colleague one day, I spoke to practically every black person in sight (a gesture which reflects my upbringing), an action which disturbed my companion. Since I addressed black folk who were clearly not associated with Yale, she wanted to know whether or not I knew them. That was funny to me. "Of course not," I answered. Yet when I thought about it seriously, I realized that in a deep way, I knew them for they, and not my companion or most of my colleagues at Yale, resemble my family. Later that year, in a black women's support group I started for undergraduates, students from poor backgrounds spoke about the shame they sometimes feel when faced with the reality of their connection to working-class and poor black people. One student confessed that her father is a street person, addicted to drugs, someone who begs from passersby. She, like other Yale students, turns away from street people often, sometimes showing anger or contempt; she hasn't wanted anyone to know that she was related to this kind of person. She struggles with this, wanting to find a way to acknowledge and affirm this reality, to claim this connection. The group asked me and one another what we [should] do to remain connected, to honor the bonds we have with working-class and poor people even as our class experience alters.

Maintaining connections with family and community across class   14
boundaries demands more than just summary recall of where one's roots are, where one comes from. It requires knowing, naming, and being ever-mindful of those aspects of one's past that have enabled and do enable one's self-development in the present, that sustain and support, that enrich. One must also honestly confront barriers that do exist, aspects of that past that do diminish. My parents' ambivalence about my love for reading led to intense conflict. They (especially my mother) would work to ensure that I had access to books, but would threaten to burn the books or throw them away if I did not conform to other expectations. Or they would insist that reading too much would drive me insane. Their ambivalence nurtured in me a like uncertainty about the value and significance of intellectual endeavor which took years for me to unlearn. While this aspect of our class reality was one that wounded and diminished, their vigilant insistence that being smart did not make me a "better" or "superior" person (which often got on my nerves because I think I wanted to have that sense that it did indeed set me apart, make me better) made a profound impression. From them I learned to value and respect various skills and talents folk might have, not just to value people who read books and talk about ideas. They and my grandparents might say about somebody, "Now he don't read nor write a lick, but he can tell a story," or as my grandmother would say, "call out the hell in words."

Empty romanticization of poor or working-class backgrounds un-   15
dermines the possibility of true connection. Such connection is based on understanding difference in experience and perspective and working to mediate and negotiate these terrains. Language is a crucial issue for folk whose movement outside the boundaries of poor and working-class backgrounds changes the nature and direction of their speech. Coming to Stanford with my own version of a Kentucky accent, which I think of always as a strong sound quite different from Tennessee or Georgia speech, I learned to speak differently while maintaining the speech of my region, the sound of my family and community. This was of course much easier to keep up when I returned home to stay often. In recent years, I have endeavored to use

various speaking styles in the classroom as a teacher and find it disconcerts those who feel that the use of a particular patois excludes them as listeners, even if there is translation into the usual, acceptable mode of speech. Learning to listen to different voices, hearing different speech challenges the notion that we must all assimilate—share a single, similar talk—in educational institutions. Language reflects the culture from which we emerge. To deny ourselves daily use of speech patterns that are common and familiar, that embody a unique and distinctive aspect of our self is one of the ways we become estranged and alienated from our past. It is important for us to have as many languages on hand as we can know or learn. It is important for those of us who are black, who speak in particular patois as well as standard English, to express ourselves in both ways.

Often I tell students from poor and working-class backgrounds that   16
if you believe what you have learned and are learning in schools and universities separates you from your past, this is precisely what will happen. It is important to stand firm in the conviction that nothing can truly separate us from our pasts when we nurture and enrich that connection. An important strategy for maintaining contact is ongoing acknowledgment of the primacy of one's past, of one's background, affirming the reality that such bonds are not severed automatically solely because one enters a new environment or moves toward a different class experience.

Again, I do not wish to romanticize this effort, to dismiss the reality   17
of conflict and contradiction. During my time at Stanford, I did go through a period of more than a year when I did not return home. That period was one where I felt that it was simply too difficult to mesh my profoundly disparate realities. Critical reflection about the choice I was making, particularly about why I felt a choice had to be made, pulled me through this difficult time. Luckily I recognized that the insistence on choosing between the world of family and community and the new world of privileged white people and privileged ways of knowing was imposed upon me by the outside. It is as though a mythical contract had been signed somewhere which demanded of us black folks that once we entered these spheres we would immediately give up all vestiges of our underprivileged past. It was my responsibility to formulate a way of being that would allow me to participate fully in my new environment while integrating and maintaining aspects of the old.

One of the most tragic manifestations of the pressure black people   18
feel to assimilate is expressed in the internalization of racist perspectives. I was shocked and saddened when I first heard black professors at Stanford downgrade and express contempt for black students, expecting us to do poorly, refusing to establish nurturing bonds. At every university I have attended as a student or worked at as a teacher, I have heard similar attitudes expressed with little or no understanding

of factors that might prevent brilliant black students from performing to their full capability. Within universities, there are few educational and social spaces where students who wish to affirm positive ties to ethnicity—to blackness, to working-class backgrounds—can receive affirmation and support. Ideologically, the message is clear—assimilation is the way to gain acceptance and approval from those in power.

Many white people enthusiastically supported Richard Rodriguez's 19 vehement contention in his autobiography, *Hunger of Memory*, that attempts to maintain ties with his Chicano background impeded his progress, that he had to sever ties with community and kin to succeed at Stanford and in the larger world, that family language, in his case Spanish, had to be made secondary or discarded. If the terms of success as defined by the standards of ruling groups within white-supremacist, capitalist patriarchy are the only standards that exist, then assimilation is indeed necessary. But they are not. Even in the face of powerful structures of domination, it remains possible for each of us, especially those of us who are members of oppressed and/or exploited groups as well as those radical visionaries who may have race, class, and sex privilege, to define and determine alternative standards, to decide on the nature and extent of compromise. Standards by which one's success is measured, whether student or professor, are quite different from those of us who wish to resist reinforcing the domination of race, sex, and class, who work to maintain and strengthen our ties with the oppressed, with those who lack material privilege, with our families who are poor and working-class.

When I wrote my first book, *Ain't I a Woman: black women and* 20 *feminism*, the issue of class and its relationship to who one's reading audience might be came up for me around my decision not to use footnotes, for which I have been sharply criticized. I told people that my concern was that footnotes set class boundaries for readers, determining who a book is for. I was shocked that many academic folk scoffed at this idea. I shared that I went into working-class black communities as well as talked with family and friends to survey whether or not they ever read books with footnotes and found that they did not. A few did not know what they were, but most folks saw them as indicating that a book was for college-educated people. These responses influenced my decision. When some of my more radical, college-educated friends freaked out about the absence of footnotes, I seriously questioned how we could ever imagine revolutionary transformation of society if such a small shift in direction could be viewed as threatening. Of course, many folks warned that the absence of footnotes would make the work less credible in academic circles. This information also highlighted the way in which class informs our choices. Certainly I did feel that choosing to use simple language, absence of footnotes, etc. would mean I was jeopardizing the possibility of being taken seriously in academic circles but then this was a political matter and a political decision.

It utterly delights me that this has proven not to be the case and that the book is read by many academics as well as by people who are not college-educated.

Always our first response when we are motivated to conform or   21 compromise within structures that reinforce domination must be to engage in critical reflection. Only by challenging ourselves to push against oppressive boundaries do we make the radical alternative possible, expanding the realm and scope of critical inquiry. Unless we share radical strategies, ways of rethinking and revisioning with students, with kin and community, with a larger audience, we risk perpetuating the stereotype that we succeed because we are the exception, different from the rest of our people. Since I left home and entered college, I am often asked, usually by white people, if my sisters and brothers are also high achievers. At the root of this question is the longing for reinforcement of the belief in "the exception" which enables race, sex, and class biases to remain intact. I am careful to separate what it means to be exceptional from a notion of "the exception."

Frequently I hear smart black folks, from poor and working-class   22 backgrounds, stressing their frustration that at times family and community do not recognize that they are exceptional. Absence of positive affirmation clearly diminishes the longing to excel in academic endeavors. Yet it is important to distinguish between the absence of basic positive affirmation and the longing for continued reinforcement that we are special. Usually liberal white folks will willingly offer continual reinforcement of us as exceptions—as special. This can be both patronizing and very seductive. Since we often work in situations where we are isolated from other black folks, we can easily begin to feel that encouragement from white people is the primary or only source of support and recognition. Given the internalization of racism, it is easy to view this support as more validating and legitimizing than similar support from black people. Still, nothing takes the place of being valued and appreciated by one's own, by one's family and community. We share a mutual and reciprocal responsibility for affirming one another's successes. Sometimes we have to talk to our folks about the fact that we need their ongoing support and affirmation, that it is unique and special to us. In some cases we may never receive desired recognition and acknowledgment of specific achievements from kin. Rather than seeing this as a basis for estrangement, for severing connection, it is useful to explore other sources of nourishment and support.

I do not know that my mother's mother ever acknowledged my college education except to ask me once, "How can you live so far away   23 from your people?" Yet she gave me sources of affirmation and nourishment, sharing the legacy of her quilt-making, of family history, of her incredible way with words. Recently, when our father retired after more than thirty years of work as a janitor, I wanted to pay tribute to this experience, to identify links between his work and my own as writer and teacher. Reflecting on our family past, I recalled ways he had been an impressive example of diligence and hard work, approaching his tasks with a seriousness and concentration I work to mirror and develop, with a discipline I struggle to maintain. Sharing these thoughts with him keeps us connected, nurtures our respect for each other, maintaining a space, however large or small, where we can talk.

Open, honest communication is the most important way we maintain relationships with kin and community as our class experience and backgrounds change. It is as vital as the sharing of resources. Often financial assistance is given in circumstances where there is no meaningful contact. However helpful, this can also be an expression of estrangement and alienation. Communication between black folks from various experiences of material privilege was much easier when we were all in segregated sharing common experiences in relation to social institutions. Without this grounding, we must work to maintain ties, connection. We must assume greater responsibility for making and maintaining contact, connections that can shape our intellectual visions and inform our radical commitments. 24

The most powerful resource any of us can have as we study and teach in university settings is full understanding and appreciation of the richness, beauty, and primacy of our familial and community backgrounds. Maintaining awareness of class differences, nurturing ties with the poor and working-class people who are our most intimate kin, our comrades in struggle, transforms and enriches our intellectual experience. Education as the practice of freedom becomes not a force which fragments or separates, but one that brings us closer, expanding our definitions of home and community. 25

QUESTIONS FOR DISCUSSION

1   Why does hooks feel both compelled to talk to her mother and intimidated by doing so? How does hooks extend the ideas exemplified in this relationship to her mother, applying it to the relationships between an educated black person and his or her community?

2   Do you agree with hooks's assumption that talking about the past and painful situations can become healing experiences? Explain your point of view.

3   Hooks's essay acknowledges and explores some of the difficulties she had remaining connected to her family and community after attending college. Why was she able to maintain a connection with her family and community? Why does she believe it is crucial for working-class people to remain connected to their pasts as they are educated in a university setting? Explain why you agree or disagree with hooks.

4   What relationships does hooks find between language and culture? Do you think she would agree or disagree with Richard Rodriguez's position on language, assimilation, and success?

5   How and why does hooks differentiate academic language from "real-world" writing? How does hooks apply the meaning of her distinction between academic and real writing in her own writing style?

IDEAS FOR WRITING

1   Hooks asserts that despite the fact that our schooling encourages us to "learn to think, write, and talk in a manner that shifts attention away from personal experience . . . we must understand that the telling of one's personal story provides a meaningful example, a way for folks to identify and connect." What are the implications of this statement? Write and essay that supports or refutes hooks's position on the need for personal narratives in effective communication.

2   Hooks argues against the assumption, which she believes prevails at universities and colleges across the country, that "assimilation is the way to gain acceptance and approval from those in power." Write an essay in support of or in opposition to hooks's position.

3   Write an essay that explores what you believe to be the two most important issues presented in this essay. Refer to hooks's text as you define each issue and then use your own experience and knowledge to develop the issue.

student essay

A Literary Debate

DAVID CHAMPLIN

Born in Mesa, Arizona in 1978, David Champlin enjoys playing the trombone, reading, running, and learning. In "A Literary Debate," Champlin brings the literary voices of the authors bell hooks and Frederick Douglass to life in a fictional discussion that explores writing as a means of communication, of persuasion, and of examining human nature.

The first battle of the War of the Words erupted at my desk one   1
February night. While sleepily plodding through a reading assignment from the education section of my writing class's course reader, I encountered a particularly well-written essay. I had the feeling that the vivid imagery and persuasive tone of the piece had come alive in my mind, manipulating my thoughts and reshaping the fundamental maxims with which I evaluated reality and society. I stopped reading and looked down at the page. Those little words seemed so powerless, trapped on their isolated sheets of paper, yet by reading them, I offered them the opportunity to invade and conquer my mind. The tiny black demons staring up at me from the book were contact mines painstakingly laid by ruthless writers, and as I read them, they leapt through my eyes and exploded in my brain, tearing my thoughts, troubling my emotions, and terrorizing my dreams. Those words were alive.

"Whoa . . . ," I mumbled as I shook my head to clear my thoughts.   2
My roommate grunted something in return as a means of saying both, "Yes, David, I feel your sleepy pain," and, "Be quiet, David, and let me finish my physics problem set in peace, or I will intensify your 'sleepy pain,'" and thus unwittingly exemplified the glorious intellectual interaction which occurs between college roommates in the dead of the night. More fatigued than I thought, I closed the course reader and used it as a pillow, comforted by the hope that those words were not really alive. . . .

". . . and down with the white-supremacist, capitalist patriarchy!"   3
screamed an angry, yet purposefully simplistic voice from a podium on page thirty-seven of the book beneath my head. "The ultimate goal of education should be inequality!"

"Miss Hooks," began a sleepy voice from a Massachusetts home on   4
page ten. "You ought to try to get some rest. I believe you meant to say, 'equality,' not 'inequality.'"

"Good evening, Mister Douglass," came hooks's steady reply. "First,   5
its hooks, not Hooks. Second, I did indeed intend to say 'inequality.'"

"Goodness, bell, why do you want to promote inequality?" objected   6
the slave-turned-scholar of the first essay of the course reader, as the
authors behind the words of the text came alive in a nocturnal debate.

"Felix E. Schelling, a U.S. educator, said in 1929 that: 7

> True education makes for inequality; the inequality of individuality, the
> inequality of success, the glorious inequality of talent, of genius; for in-
> equality, not mediocrity, individual superiority, not standardization, is the
> measure of the progress of the world.

Education of the masses betters society as a whole by helping individuals to realize their potential for intellectual, social, and moral growth.
When we focus on developing the special talents of each individual,
inequality closely follows education. In a broader cultural sense, inequality ensures the continued defense of social class and heritage
that make our society diverse. We should be proud of our differences,
and we should not allow education to try to smear our backgrounds
into a mush-colored mixture of assimilated immigrant traditions."

Douglass, somewhat bewildered by this radically unique perspec-   8
tive on education and its effect on equality, thought a moment. "I
noticed, bell, that in your writing you often argued for the preservation of class heritage as well as ethnic or social heritage. Why do you
want to keep impoverished, uneducated groups of people in their low
social positions?"

"Who is to say that belonging to a higher social position makes an   9
individual a better person?" came the reply. "Why must a person be
concerned with 'advancing' in society if he or she is content to live the
way that he or she lives? Education should not force people to change
their way of life or be ashamed of their background. Education should
provide people with the tools necessary for interacting with others
and with information about the choices that they have in society. We
should educate society's youth about the values of differences between human beings without making a judgment concerning which
group is the 'correct' group that should be emulated. . . ."

"Why do people always decide to talk loudly whenever I try to go to   10
sleep?" I wondered as I briefly opened my eyes to blink at the clock on
my desk. Without moving my head from the course reader, I groggily
scanned the room for the boisterous debaters. My subconscious mind
thoroughly enjoyed the debate raging between the covers of the text-
book, and in my delirious state of slumber, decided to share its en-
thusiasm with the rest of my psyche. "See, that's the interesting thing
about writing, Dave," my subconscious tried to tell my snoring self.
"The medium of literature allows for intergenerational debate between the authors and ideas of different times. Authors' ideas are
forever preserved in the words they leave for the future, and once read
by a later audience, those ideas are brought back to life. Think of it as

a resuscitation of an intellect. Perhaps we could say that writing is a
means to achieve immortality." After looking around the room and
finding only my drowsy roommate, I rolled my head off the reader
towards the edge of my desk and fell back asleep. . . .

"Oh, and Frederick," hooks continued, "please do something about   11
your voice. Your passage up there in front of the course reader is written in an intellectual, elevated tone. In your first paragraph alone, you
employ such scholarly words as, 'compelled,' 'resort,' 'stratagems,'
'commenced,' 'depravity,' and 'indispensable.' If you want to be able
to connect with an uneducated audience in order to inform them of
the ideas you express, and thereby educate them, you must speak in a
language that they feel comfortable with. As I say in my essay, 'To
speak with language that is accessible to as many folks as possible
is . . . important.' How effective do you think your writing was at
reaching, and not alienating, your fellow slaves?"

"Should the writer focus on speaking at a level which the reader   12
feels comfortable with, or should one use more elevated, sophisticated speech when communicating with one's fellow man?" replied
Douglass. "I choose to use advanced speech, as I believe that the audience which sees and hears higher levels of knowledge will gradually
become accustomed to that higher level of intellectual interaction
and will learn by merely listening to another person speak. Where did
you learn most of your writing skills, bell?"

"I suppose I learned from reading books in my childhood."   13

"By reading material that was probably written above you own level   14
of understanding, you learned grammar and vocabulary. You may have
struggled with a few words and concepts, but education is not necessarily a 'comfortable' experience. It may be rightly said, in fact, that discomfort not only increases the retention of knowledge but is necessary
for learning to occur. In my passage, I describe the agony I experienced
when my newfound knowledge finally revealed the hideousness of the
condition of those enslaved in the South. In addition, it is true that
people 'learn from mistakes.' Why is this an educational process?"

"Because when people err," responded hooks, "they experience   15
unpleasant outcomes, like embarrassment and reprimands, which
they would rather not experience in the future. But, Frederick, that is
a very negative approach to learning. . . ."

"Yeah, and talking loudly while I'm trying to sleep is a good way to   16
make me take a negative approach to my day tomorrow," my semi-
conscious psyche retorted. As my body rolled itself farther away from
that noisy course reader, my subconscious returned to its earlier train
of thought, ". . . and what does writing's unique ability to transcend
time and culture mean? Obviously, we can view writing as a vehicle
which transports us to different times so that we might learn about
the past. . . ."

"Is there anything you liked about my writing, bell?" asked Douglass.   17

"I thought your use of personal examples was quite effective in   18
drawing the reader deeper into your writing so that he or she could
feel your suffering and identify with your struggle to gain literacy."

"Yes, I noticed that you employ such examples in your own writing.   19
Now, I view education as a means of acquiring intellectual and physical freedom. When I first realized what it meant to be enslaved, I
compared my state with that of my master and other freemen. I realized that our positions in society were unequal."

"Good!" exclaimed bell.   20

"No, not good. Being equal meant being just as free to control one's   21
own life as every other person in the nation, having the freedom to
nourish one's body, mind, and soul without having to fear the hatred of
hostile social groups, and being evaluated by one's merits instead of
one's heritage or social position. Existing in a state of inequality meant
slavery, suffering, and submission of the intellect, as a group of people
endeavored to exploit the natural differences between humans for their
personal profit. Education gives one the power to recognize inequality
and injustice in a society. In the words of Lord Brougham, a Scottish
jurist of the nineteenth century, 'Education makes a people easy to
lead, but difficult to drive; easy to govern but impossible to enslave.' . . ."

In my attempt to find a silent spot for my heavy head, I had rolled   22
out to the very edge of the desk. Unaware of its imminent peril, my
subconscious continued its soliloquy inside my mind. "At a more
complex level, we find that different authors in different times often
address the same issues in their works. Take, for example, the commonality of themes of shaping education, acquiring and maintaining
freedom, and struggling through racism which define the works by
Douglass and hooks. This continuity or universality of certain societal
themes in works written in different time periods seems to offer proof
that there are some facets of civilization that have remained constant
throughout the ages. By examining those recurring concepts or societal woes, we discover eternal characteristics of human nature. Our
study of past literature, then, becomes an examination of the degree
of success past societies had at recognizing and moderating the natural desires of human nature." I wrestled with strange dreams as my
nose reached out over the abyss beyond the edge of the desk. . . .

"On the fourth page of your essay, bell," Douglass resumed, "you   23
retell the story of your college experience. At one point you criticize
your peers for their questioning of the values held by their parents
and by society. Is questioning the structure of the society in which one
lives not an integral part of the learning process? College is a period of
time when the student is supposed to be exposed to new ideas from
many diverse schools of thought. One of the most fundamental purposes of the university is to teach youths to objectively evaluate and

question new ideas in search for a greater understanding, and it is only through the exposure of a wide base of information including arguments from both sides of a topic that one can begin to make educated decisions. Education, then, cannot be devoid of the questioning of our environment. Without this questioning of society, there would be no societal change or improvement. If people on both sides of the thirty-seventh parallel had not questioned the morality of slavery, that dreadful institution might still exist. . . ."

Feeling itself nearing a universal truth, my eager subconscious resumed, ". . . by studying literature, then, we study the ideas of the past. By examining the ideas which shaped the societies of the past, we can discover how each society developed a system for controlling human nature. From this analysis of what made one society more successful than another in coping with fundamental characteristics of the human species, we can better decide how to shape our present society. To fully make use of our written resources, we must study the ideas of the past and incorporate them in our views of the future. . . ."   24

"I see your point, Frederick," began hooks, "but I also see education which pursues equality as the ultimate goal as being a threat to the existence of the traditions of distinct societal groups. Perhaps a compromise between our philosophies is the best solution."   25

"Yes, we should seek education which empowers people without insulting their heritage. Education, then, should be directed toward exposing people to the diversity which characterizes human thought and experience so that citizens are able to make informed choices while leading socially responsible lives, and so that they respect and cherish the differences which enrich the human community."   26

In my final attempt to escape the noise of the conversation, I rolled my head farther to the left and into that empty space which begins where the tops of desks end. As my face plummeted towards a gruesome clutter of pencils, problem sets, and textbooks strewn on the floor, my subconscious mind had just enough time to realize, "Ideas that never reach expression on paper die with the humans who think them, but ideas that are written are immortal. Thus, ideas, and the written words that express them, possess immense power. Written ideas shape not only the society into which they are born, but civilization for all time thereafter. It is our duty as readers to harness this power so that we may use it to enrich the society in which we live. As writers, we have a duty to share our knowledge with future generations, and an opportunity to make our thoughts live forever. Words *are* powerful!" An instant later, my thoughts were obliterated by a close encounter with the cover of my physics book. A strange laughter erupted from my calculus notes lying nearby as the linguistic invasion led by words exercising their power claimed its first victim.   27

1   Do you think David Champlin's dialogic method of exploring the differences between hooks's and Douglass's thinking about education is effective? Explain.

2   What other educational issues do you think hooks and Douglass might debate?

3   Both hooks and Douglass discuss the impact of social and cultural values on the way in which educational institutions and curricula are developed and shaped. What impact do you think social changes have on educational institutions?

4   Do you think it should be a major function of educational institutions to encourage the acceptance of cultural, social, and economic differences? Why or why not?

5   Does an educated person have a responsibility to his or her family and culture to raise the awareness of the community and try to change unjust conditions?

IDEAS FOR WRITING

1   What social values do you think public education should support? Write an essay in which you present and support your point of view; refer to hooks, Douglass, and Champlin (or other writers in this anthology) when relevant.

2   Write an imaginary but probable debate between two of the writers in this anthology over an educational issue, such as bilingual education, the need for a common curriculum, or the role of testing and discipline in a classroom.

Thinking About How We Learn

Multiple Intelligences

HOWARD GARDNER

*Howard Gardner is best known for his theory of multiple intelli-
gences and for his individualized and humanistic approach to education: "My feeling is that assessment can be much broader, much more
humane than it is now, and that psychologists should spend less time
ranking people and more time trying to help them." Gardner, the
author of fifteen books on learning and the mind, has been involved
in school reform since 1983, when his theory of multiple intelligences
was first presented in* Frames of Mind. *A professor of education and
adjunct professor of psychology at Harvard, Howard Gardner is the
codirector of Project Zero, a research group in human cognition that
has a special focus on the arts. His most widely read books include*
The Mind's New Science *(1985),* The Unschooled Mind *(1991), and*
Leading Minds: An Anatomy of Leadership *(1996). The selection
that follows is excerpted from* Frames of Mind.

Allow me to transport all of us to the Paris of 1900—La Belle Epoque—   1
when the city fathers of Paris approached a psychologist named Alfred
Binet with an unusual request: Could he devise some kind of a measure that would predict which youngsters would succeed and which
would fail in the primary grades of Paris schools? As everybody knows,
Binet succeeded. In short order, his discovery came to be called the
"intelligence test"; his measure, the "IQ." Like other Parisian fashions,
the IQ soon made its way to the United States, where it enjoyed a mod-
est success until World War I. Then, it was used to test over one million
American recruits, and it had truly arrived. From that day on, the IQ
test has looked like psychology's biggest success—a genuinely useful
scientific tool.

What is the vision that led to the excitement about IQ? At least in   2
the West, people had always relied on intuitive assessments of how
smart other people were. Now intelligence seemed to be quantifiable.
You could measure someone's actual or potential height, and now, it
seemed, you could also measure someone's actual or potential intelligence. We had one dimension of mental ability along which we could
array everyone.

The search for the perfect measure of intelligence has proceeded   3
apace. Here, for example, are some quotations from an ad for a widely
used test:

> Need an individual test which quickly provides a stable and reliable esti-
> mate of intelligence in four or five minutes per form? Has three forms?
> Does not depend on verbal production or subjective scoring? Can be used
> with the severely handicapped (even paralyzed) if they can signal yes or

no? Handles two-year-olds and superior adults with the same short series of items and the same format? Only $16.00 complete.

Now, that's quite a claim. The American psychologist Arthur Jensen   4
suggests that we could look at reaction time to assess intelligence: a set of lights go on; how quickly can the subject react? The British psychologist Hans Eysenck suggests that investigators of intelligence should look directly at brain waves.

There are also, of course, more sophisticated versions of the IQ test.   5
One of them is called the Scholastic Aptitude Test (SAT). It purports to be a similar kind of measure, and if you add up a person's verbal and math scores, as is often done, you can rate him or her along a single intellectual dimension. Programs for the gifted, for example, often use that kind of measure; if your IQ is in excess of 130, you're admitted to the program.

I want to suggest that along this one-dimensional view of how to as-   6
sess people's minds comes a corresponding view of school, which I will call the "uniform view." In the uniform school, there is a core curriculum, a set of facts that everybody should know, and very few electives. The better students, perhaps those with higher IQs, are allowed to take courses that call upon critical reading, calculation, and thinking skills. In the "uniform school," there are regular assessments using paper and pencil instruments, of the IQ or SAT variety. They yield reliable rankings of people; the best and the brightest get into the better colleges, and perhaps—but only perhaps—they will also get better rankings in life. There is no question but that this approach works well for certain people—schools such as Harvard are eloquent testimony to that. Since this measurement and selection system is clearly meritocratic in certain respects, it has something to recommend it.

But there is an alternative vision that I would like to present—one   7
based on a radically different view of the mind, and one that yields a very different view of school. It is a pluralistic view of mind, recognizing many different and discrete facets of cognition, acknowledging that people have different cognitive strengths and contrasting cognitive styles. I would also like to introduce the concept of an individual-centered school that takes this multifaceted view of intelligence seriously. This model for a school is based in part on findings from sciences that did not even exist in Binet's time: cognitive science (the study of the mind), and neuroscience (the study of the brain). One such approach I have called my "theory of multiple intelligences." Let me tell you something about its sources, its claims, and its educational implications for a possible school of the future.

Dissatisfaction with the concept of IQ and with unitary views of   8
intelligence is fairly widespread—one thinks, for instance, of the work of L. L. Thurstone, J. P. Guilford, and other critics. From my point of view, however, these criticisms do not suffice. The whole concept has to be challenged; in fact, it has to be replaced.

I believe that we should get away altogether from tests and corre- 9
lations among tests, and look instead at more naturalistic sources of
information about how peoples around the world develop skills
important to their way of life. Think, for example, of sailors in the
South Seas, who find their way around hundreds, or even thousands,
of islands by looking at the constellations of stars in the sky, feeling
the way a boat passes over the water, and noticing a few scattered
landmarks. A word for intelligence in a society of these sailors would
probably refer to that kind of navigational ability. Think of surgeons
and engineers, hunters and fishermen, dancers and choreographers,
athletes and athletic coaches, tribal chiefs and sorcerers. All of these
different roles need to be taken into account if we accept the way I
define intelligence—that is, as the ability to solve problems, or to
fashion products, that are valued in one or more cultural or community settings. For the moment I am saying nothing about whether
there is one dimension, or more than one dimension, of intelligence;
nothing about whether intelligence is inborn or developed. Instead I
emphasize the ability to solve problems and to fashion products. In
my work I seek the building blocks of the intelligences used by the
aforementioned sailors and surgeons and sorcerers.

The science in this enterprise, to the extent that it exists, involves 10
trying to discover the *right* description of the intelligences. What is an
intelligence? To try to answer this question, I have, with my colleagues,
surveyed a wide set of sources which, to my knowledge, have never
been considered together before. One source is what we already know
concerning the development of different kinds of skills in normal
children. Another source, and a very important one, is information on
the ways that these abilities break down under conditions of brain
damage. When one suffers a stroke or some other kind of brain damage, various abilities can be destroyed, or spared, in isolation from
other abilities. This research with brain-damaged patients yields a very
powerful kind of evidence, because it seems to reflect the way the
nervous system has evolved over the millennia to yield certain discrete
kinds of intelligence.

My research group looks at other special populations as well: 11
prodigies, idiot savants, autistic children, children with learning dis-
abilities, all of whom exhibit very jagged cognitive profiles—profiles
that are extremely difficult to explain in terms of a unitary view of
intelligence. We examine cognition in diverse animal species and in
dramatically different cultures. Finally, we consider two kinds of psychological evidence: correlations among psychological tests of the
sort yielded by a careful statistical analysis of a test battery; and the
results of efforts of skill training. When you train a person in skill
A, for example, does that training transfer to skill B? So, for example,
does training in mathematics enhance one's musical abilities, or
vice versa?

Obviously, through looking at all these sources—information on   12
development, on breakdowns, on special populations, and the like—
we end up with a cornucopia of information. Optimally, we would
perform a statistical factor analysis, feeding all the data into a com-
puter and noting the kinds of factors or intelligences that are ex-
tracted. Alas, the kind of material with which I was working didn't
exist in a form that is susceptible to computation, and so we had to
perform a more subjective factor analysis. In truth, we simply studied
the results as best we could, and tried to organize them in a way that
made sense to us, and hopefully, to critical readers as well. My result-
ing list of seven intelligences is a preliminary attempt to organize this
mass of information.

I want now to mention briefly the seven intelligences we have   13
located, and to cite one or two examples of each intelligence. Linguistic intelligence is the kind of ability exhibited in its fullest form, perhaps, by poets. Logical-mathematical intelligence, as the name implies,
is logical and mathematical ability, as well as scientific ability. Jean
Piaget, the great developmental psychologist, though he was studying
all intelligence, but I believe he was studying the development of
logical-mathematical intelligence. Although I name the linguistic and
logical-mathematical intelligences first, it is not because I think they
are most important—in fact, I am convinced that all seven of the
intelligences have equal priority. In our society, however, we have
put linguistic and logical-mathematical intelligences, figuratively
speaking, on a pedestal. Much of our testing is based on this high val-
uation of verbal and mathematical skills. If you do well in language
and logic, you should do well in IQ tests and SATs, and you may well
get into a prestigious college, but whether you do well once you leave
is probably going to depend as much on the extent to which you
posses and use the other intelligences, and it is to those that I want to
give equal attention.

Spatial intelligence is the ability to form a mental model of a spa-   14
tial world and to be able to maneuver and operate using that model.
Sailors, engineers, surgeons, sculptors, and painters, to name just a
few examples, all have highly developed spatial intelligence. Musical
intelligence is the fourth category of ability we have identified:
Leonard Bernstein had lots of it; Mozart, presumably, had even more.
Bodily-kinesthetic intelligence is the ability to solve problems or to
fashion products using one's whole body, or parts of the body.
Dancers, athletes, surgeons, and craftspeople all exhibit highly developed bodily-kinesthetic intelligence.

Finally, I propose two forms of personal intelligence—not well un-   15
derstood, elusive to study, but immensely important. Interpersonal
intelligence is the ability to understand other people: what motivates
them, how they work, how to work cooperatively with them. Successful salespeople, politicians, teachers, clinicians, and religious leaders

are all likely to be individuals with high degrees of interpersonal intelligence. Intrapersonal intelligence, a seventh kind of intelligence, is a correlative ability, turned inward. It is a capacity to form an accurate, veridical model of oneself and to be able to use that model to operate effectively in life.

These, then, are the seven intelligences that we have uncovered and described in our research. This is a preliminary list, as I have said; obviously, each form of intelligence can be subdivided, or the list can be rearranged. The real point here is to make the case for the plurality of the intellect. Also, we believe that individuals may differ in the particular intelligence profiles with which they are born, and that certainly they differ in the profiles they end up with. I think of intelligences as raw, biological potentials, which can be seen in pure form only in individuals who are, in the technical sense, freaks. In almost everybody else the intelligences work together to solve problems, to yield various kinds of cultural endstates—vocations, avocations, and the like. 16

This is my theory of multiple intelligences in capsule form. In my view, the purpose of school should be to develop intelligences and to help people reach vocational and avocational goals that are appropriate to their particular spectrum of intelligences. People who are helped to do so, I believe, feel more engaged and competent, and therefore more inclined to serve the society in a constructive way. 17

These thoughts, and the critique of a universalistic view of the mind with which I began, lead to the notion of an individual-centered school, one geared to optimal understanding and development of each student's cognitive profile. This vision stands in direct contrast to that of the uniform school that I described earlier. 18

The design of my ideal school of the future is based upon two assumptions. The first is that not all people have the same interests and abilities; not all of us learn in the same way. (And we now have the tools to begin to address these individual differences in school.) The second assumption is one that hurts: it is the assumption that nowadays no one person can learn everything there is to learn. We would all like, as Renaissance men and women, to know everything, or at least to believe in the potential of knowing everything, but that ideal clearly is not possible anymore. Choice is therefore inevitable, and one of the things I want to argue is that the choices that we make for ourselves, and for the people who are under our charge, might as well be informed choices. An individual-centered school would be rich in assessment of individual abilities and proclivities. It would seek to match individuals not only to curricular areas, but also to particular ways of teaching those subjects. And after the first few grades, the school would also seek to match individuals with the various kinds of life and work options that are available in their culture. 19

I want to propose a new set of roles for educators that might make this vision a reality. First of all, we might have what I will call 20 "assessment specialists." The job of these people would be to try to understand as sensitively and comprehensively as possible the abilities and interests of the students in a school. It would be very important, however, that the assessment specialists use "intelligence-fair" instruments. We want to be able to look specifically and directly at spatial abilities, at personal abilities, and the like, and not through the usual lenses of the linguistic and logical-mathematical intelligences. Up until now nearly all assessment has depended indirectly on measurement of those abilities; if students are not strong in those two areas, their abilities in other areas may be obscured. Once we begin to try to assess other kinds of intelligences directly, I am confident that particular students will reveal strengths in quite different areas, and the notion of general brightness will disappear or become greatly attenuated.

21   In addition to the assessment specialist, the school of the future might have the "student-curriculum broker." It would be his or her job to help match students' profiles, goals, and interests to particular curricula and to particular styles of learning. Incidentally, I think that the new interactive technologies offer considerable promise in this area: it will probably be much easier in the future for "brokers" to match individual students to ways of learning that prove comfortable for them.

22   There should also be, I think, a "school-community broker," who would match students to learning opportunities in the wider community. It would be this person's job to find situations in the community, particularly options not available in the school, for children who exhibit unusual cognitive profiles. I have in mind apprenticeships, mentorships, internships in organizations, "big brothers," "big sisters"—individuals and organizations with whom these students might work to secure a feeling for different kinds of vocational and avocational roles in the society. I am not worried about those occasional youngsters who are good in everything. They're going to do just fine. I'm concerned about those who don't shine in the standardized tests, and who, therefore, tend to be written off as not having gifts of any kind. It seems to me that the school-community broker could spot these youngsters and find placements in the community that provide chances for them to shine.

23   There is ample room in this vision for teachers, as well, and also for master teachers. In my view, teachers would be freed to do what they are supposed to do, which is to teach their subject matter, in their preferred style of teaching. The job of master teacher would be very demanding. It would involve, first of all, supervising the novice teachers and guiding them; but the master teacher would also seek to ensure that the complex student-assessment-curriculum-community equation is balanced appropriately. If the equation is seriously imbalanced, master teachers would intervene and suggest ways to make things better.

24   Clearly, what I am describing is a tall order; it might even be called utopian. And there is a major risk to this program, of which I am well

aware. That is the risk of premature billeting—of saying, "Well, Johnny is four, he seems to be musical, so we are going to send him to Juilliard and drop everything else." There is, however, nothing inherent in the approach that I have described that demands this early overdetermination—quite the contrary. It seems to me that early identification of strengths can be very helpful in indicating what kinds of experiences children might profit from; but early identification of weaknesses can be equally important. If a weakness is identified early, there is a chance to attend to it before it is too late, and to come up with alternative ways of teaching or of covering an important skill area.

We now have the technological and the human resources to implement such an individual-centered school. Achieving it is a question of will, including the will to withstand the current enormous pressures toward uniformity and unidimensional assessments. There are strong pressures now, which you read about every day in the newspapers to compare students, to compare teachers, states, even entire countries, using one dimension or criterion, a kind of crypto-IQ assessment. Clearly, everything I have described today stands in direct opposition to that particular view of the world. Indeed that is my intent—to provide a ringing indictment of such one-track thinking.   25

I believe that in our society we suffer from three biases, which I have nicknamed "Westist," "Testist," and "Bestist." "Westist" involves putting certain Western cultural values, which date back to Socrates, on a pedestal. Logical thinking, for example, is important; rationality is important; but they are not the only virtues. "Testist" suggests a bias towards focusing upon those human abilities or approaches that are readily testable. If it can't be tested, it sometimes seems, it is not worth paying attention to. My feeling is that assessment can be much broader, much more humane than it is now, and that psychologists should spend less time ranking people and more time trying to help them.   26

"Bestist" is a not very veiled reference to a book by David Halberstam called *The Best and the Brightest*. Halberstam referred ironically to figures such as Harvard faculty members who were brought to Washington to help President John F. Kennedy and in the process launched the Vietnam War. I think that any belief that all the answers to a given problem lie in one certain approach, such as logical-mathematical thinking, can be very dangerous. Current views of intellect need to be leavened with other more comprehensive points of view.   27

It is of the utmost importance that we recognize and nurture all of the varied human intelligences, and all of the combinations of intelligences. We are all so different largely because we have different combinations of intelligences. If we recognize this, I think we will have at least a better chance of dealing appropriately with the many problems that we face in the world. If we can mobilize the spectrum of human abilities, not only will people feel better about themselves and more competent; it is even possible that they will also feel more   28 engaged and better able to join the rest of the world community in working for the broader good. Perhaps if we can mobilize the full range of human intelligences and ally them to an ethical sense, we can help to increase the likelihood of our survival on this planet, and perhaps even contribute to our thriving.

QUESTIONS FOR DISCUSSION

1   Based on your own experience and that of your family and friends, are you in agreement with Gardner's critique of the "one-dimensional view" of how to assess intelligence and potential? Explain your position.

2   Identify and discuss three argumentative strategies that Gardner uses in his essay. Is his argument a valid and convincing one?

3   Why does Gardner connect a one-dimensional view of intelligence to a uniform or core curriculum. Do you accept his logic and agree with his claim? Explain.

4   What type of research does Gardner conduct before establishing his seven forms of intelligence? Do you think that his research strategy can and does lead to a convincing theory? Are you skeptical of his research strategies, his way of assessing his evidence, or his conclusions?

5   Why is Gardner opposed to the biases in education today reflected by "Westist," "Testist," and "Bestist"? Do you agree or disagree with him? Why does Gardner believe that his approach to educating people will help to build stronger communities? Do you agree or disagree with him? Explain.

IDEAS FOR WRITING

1   Write an essay that supports or refutes Gardner's definition of intelligence.

2   Write an essay that supports or refutes Gardner's notion of an individual-centered school, one geared to optimal understanding and development of each student's cognitive profile.

The Common School and the Common Good

E. D. HIRSCH, JR.

E. D. Hirsch, Jr. has had a major impact on America's national approach to teaching our children. He was born in Tennessee in 1928, and earned his B.A. from Cornell in 1950, and his Ph.D. from Yale in 1957. Hirsch has won many distinguished fellowships, including the Guggenheim and the Fulbright. As the Linden Kent Memorial Professor of English and University Professor of Education and Humanities at the University of Virginia and a Fellow of the Institute for Advanced Study in the Social Sciences at Stanford, Hirsch developed his theory that a "core body of knowledge is a way of promoting economic justice through education." His ideas are best summarized in his controversial national bestseller Cultural Literacy: What Every American Needs to Know *(1987). In the following selection, which is excerpted from his most recent book,* The Schools We Need and Why We Don't Have Them *(1996), Hirsch argues for the necessity of implementing a core curriculum.*

Every nation that manages to achieve universal readiness in the early grades for all its children—a few examples are France, Hungary, Norway, Japan, Korea, Sweden, and Denmark—does so by following grade-by-grade standards. In large, diverse nations as well as small, homogenous ones, a common core curriculum appears to be the only practical means for achieving universal readiness at each grade level. Universal readiness, in turn, is the only means for achieving universal competence and for combining excellence with fairness. In contrast, no nation that *dispenses* with grade-by-grade standards has managed to achieve universal readiness, excellence, and fairness. The Netherlands, for example, is a non-core-curriculum nation that has managed to attain a high average level of excellence because of very high achievement among the top half of its students, but it has failed to achieve universal competence and fairness. Indeed, the Netherlands, the only non-core-curriculum nation of Northern Europe, exhibits the lowest degree of educational fairness in that region, with some 16 percent of its schools falling below minimum competency, as contrasted with about 2.5 percent among its core-curriculum neighbors. (The United States figure is 30 percent of schools below minimum competency.)

An informative exception to this correlation is found in Switzerland, which lacks a national core curriculum but achieves the best combination of excellence and fairness in the world, having the highest average level of achievement coupled with the smallest standard deviation. But on closer inspection, we find that in fact Switzerland has one of the most detailed and demanding core curriculums in the world, with each canton specifying in detail the minimum knowledge and skill that each child achieve in each grade, and an accountability system that ensures the attainment of those universal standards. There is some commonality in standards among the cantons, but equally important, Swiss children rarely move from one canton to another in the course of their schooling. Each child therefore receives a highly coherent, carefully monitored sequence of early learnings such as children receive in countries that have grade-by-grade standards nationwide.

To the reader who may feel that these international data have little   3
relevance to the United States, with its anticentralized educational traditions and its diversity, the Swiss example, in which each state fixes its own core curriculum, may appear to have the greatest affinity with our own tradition of state and local control. That would be the case, however, only if our children did not move so frequently from one school to another, and stayed put as the Swiss do. In the 1930s, William Bagley summarized the problem of American nomadism (which has grown more acute since he wrote):

> The notion that each community must have a curriculum all its own is not only silly, but tragic. It neglects two important needs. The first, as we have already seen, is the need of a democracy for many common elements in the culture of all people, to the end that the people may discuss collective problems in terms that will convey common meanings. The second need is extremely practical. It is the need of recognizing the fact that American people simply will not "stay put." They are the most mobile people in the world. . . . Under these conditions, failure to have a goodly measure of uniformity in school subjects and grade placement is a gross injustice to at least ten million school children at the present time.

The injustice that Bagley identified has intensified for many   4
reasons, and it now extends to many more than ten million children. The average inner-city mobility rates (the percentage of children in a school who transfer in or out during the school year) lie routinely between 45 and 80 percent. Some inner-city school have mobility rates of over 100 percent. A recent analysis from the United States General Accounting Office reported that one sixth of all third graders attend at least three schools between first and third grade. Given the curricular incoherence of schooling even for those who stay at the same school, the fragmentation and incoherence of the education provided to frequently moving students are heartbreaking.

In sum, the high mobility of our children, especially of those who   5
can least afford educational disruption, makes common learnings *more* needed in the United States than in most other nations. The argument that we are different from others and require different educational arrangements points to more, not less, commonality in our educational standards. It is certainly true that we cannot reasonably

be compared to Switzerland, but our children's high mobility rates are all the more reason why we cannot reasonably follow the Swiss principle of isolated localism. Our diversity, size, and nomadism are arguments in favor of, not against, common, grade-by-grade standards. Until very recently, of course, the idea of common standards in the United States has been unthinkable among American educational experts. Localism remains a quasi-sacred principle, despite the fact that few localities actually impose explicit content standards. But many people are coming to feel that, considering the glaring knowledge gaps and boring repetitions that children experience even when they stay at the same school, continuing our educational incoherence, nonaccountability, and inequity would be even more unthinkable.

Bagley's other point, that common learnings are necessary to a functioning democracy, is an educational principle that has been accepted in most democracies of the world, including our own in its earlier years. The institution of the common school, proposed by Jefferson and fostered by Horace Mann, had the goal of giving all children the shared intellectual and social capital that would enable them to participate as autonomous citizens in the economy and policy of the nation. When Jefferson said that if he had to choose between newspapers and the government, he would choose newspapers, he went on to say that his remark was premised on each citizen's being able to read and understand the newspapers. It was a prescient addendum. A citizenry cannot read and understand newspapers, much less participate effectively in a modern economy, without sharing the common intellectual capital that makes understanding and communication possible. In a large, diverse nation, the common school is the only institution available for creating a school-based culture that, like a common language, enables everyone to communicate in the public sphere.

The principle that children should enter a new grade already sharing the background knowledge required to understand the teacher and each other is at bottom the principle that enables the functioning of an entire community or nation. People cannot effectively meet in the classroom or in the marketplace unless they can communicate with and learn from each another. It is the duty of a nation's educational system to create this domain of public communicability. It cannot do so without the common school, and the common school cannot be truly such without providing each child the shared intellectual capital that will be needed in each early grade, and needed ultimately in society after graduation. A shared public culture that enables public communicability is essential to an effective community at every age and stage of life, and most emphatically in the early grades, when deficits can be made up. Once out of school, a citizen must continue to share the common intellectual capital of the nation in order to communicate and learn.

The need to develop and nurture this cultural commons was 8
implicitly understood by the founders, and is consistent with their
motivation for having a First Amendment clause that forbids the establishment of a state religion. Divisiveness was to be excluded from
the cultural commons. Guided by the principle of public toleration
enunciated by John Locke and others after the bloody seventeenth-
century wars of religion, the founders desired that the laws and customs of the public sphere should favor no single sect but should
promote the general welfare. Customs divisive and dangerous to the
internal peace of the nation, chiefly sectarian religions, were to be
relegated to the private sphere, enabling all to meet in the public
sphere as fellow citizens and equals. The deliberately artificial wall of
separation helped create and nurture a public domain of toleration
and civility, while leaving everyone as free as possible in their private
lives. It was a brilliant Enlightenment political innovation for encour-
aging internal peace and solidarity in a large nation, and it led to the
development of a uniquely American public culture. The development of this cosmopolitan culture was thus no accident. It had been
openly discussed in the later Enlightenment, notably in the writings
of Immanuel Kant. In the minds of Jefferson, Mann, and other democratic theorists in France and elsewhere, the common school was to
be not just the instrument of knowledge, literacy, and equality of opportunity but also the agent of a cosmopolitan culture that would
promote universal respect and civility.

In our own day, the chief danger to this ecumenical, cosmopolitan 9
public culture is not a religious but an ethnic sectarianism. The two
kinds of sect, religious and ethnic, are highly similar in their divisiveness and their danger to the shared public sphere. Had the idea of
ethnic strife been as present in the minds of the Founding Fathers as
the idea of religious strife, our founding laws might have included a
clause forbidding the establishment of a narrow ethnic culture. Just as
the invocations of the Divinity in our public ceremonies are deliberately nonsectarian, hybrid affairs, engaged in by rabbis as well as
priests, so our public culture is a hybrid construct that contains het-
erogeneous elements from various ethnic groups. Recently, Orlando
Patterson has spoken of "cross-pollinating our multi-ethnic communities" in order to "promote that precious overarching national
culture—the envy of the world—which I call ecumenical America."
But Patterson sees a serious danger to that overarching culture in

> balkanizing America both intellectually and culturally. One has only to
> walk for a few minutes on any large campus (the unfortunate coales-
> cence of the left separatists and the right republican anti-communitarian
> individualists/separatists!) to witness the pervasiveness of ethnic separa-
> tism, marked by periodic outbursts of other chauvinisms and hostilities.

Patterson urges instead a return to the cosmopolitan ideal of the commons:

> Universities and businesses should return to the principle of integration, to the notion that diversity is not something to be celebrated and promoted in its own right, but an opportunity for mutual understanding and the furtherance of an ecumenical national culture.

Patterson and others, notably Arthur Schlesinger, Jr., have been urging that the principle of multiculturalism should be guided into this ecumenical, cosmopolitan direction for the good of the nation rather than fostering its all-too-prevalent tendency toward angry separatism and mutual hostility. This book strongly supports that view. Whether multiculturalism should be given a Romantic, separatist form (in the tradition of Fichte) or an Enlightenment, cosmopolitan form (in the tradition of Kant) has an obvious bearing on the educational question of common learnings in the early grades. In my view, the Romantic version of ethnicity is as deleterious to public education as the Romantic conception of pedagogy. The common learnings taught in school should promote a cosmopolitan, ecumenical, hybrid public culture in which all meet on an equal footing—a culture that is as deliberately artificial and nonsectarian as our public invocations of the Divinity. This school-based culture belongs to everyone and to no one. Its function is analogous to that of the hybrid lingua francas of the medieval marketplace, which were the antecedents of the major national languages—themselves hybrid, artificially constructed affairs, mostly codified by committees.

In the United States, the process of reaching agreement about a sequence of common learnings in the early grades is likely to be lengthy, conflict-ridden, and, at the start, unofficial. A highly specific common core of content is still repellent to many Americans. Gradually, however, general agreement on such a core might be developed if the public and the educational community became fully persuaded that some degree of grade-by-grade commonality is necessary to educational excellence and equity. (A 50 percent common core has proved to be acceptable to parents in Core Knowledge schools.) The public will be all the more likely to reach this conclusion when it becomes more fully aware that the educational formalism has turned the jealously guarded principle of local curriculum control into a myth. As far as specific content is concerned, the local curriculum, with few exceptions, does not exist. One cannot reasonably endorse something that does not exist, though one can demand that it come into existence. If the public simply insisted upon a true common core of learnings at the local level, that would mark a huge advance in our educational arrangements, and might in time lead to still broader commonalities.

Because this book has been focused mainly on kindergarten through grade eight—decisive grades for determining the excellence and equity of schooling—I have paid scant attention to high school. That is a conscious omission. If the principles of early education advanced here were to be followed, American high schools would change perforce for the better. Their incoming students would have already received the foundational knowledge and skill needed for good citizenship. (In earlier eras, many exemplary citizens-to-be were compelled to leave school by the end of grade eight.) Students would not need to be shepherded into so many elementary courses; they could follow more varied and intensive strands of academic or vocational study according to their interests and abilities. As a consequence, the American high school would become a more interesting and effective place for all types of students.

Beyond urging agreement at the local level, I have not made any   13
suggestions regarding the large-scale policies needed to create more demanding elementary schools. I haven't answered questions like What shall we do tomorrow? and Who shall be in charge? The possible administrative means for accomplishing the task are many, but there can be no substitute for the main elements of the task itself. Schools need to have a coherent, cumulative core curriculum which instills consensus values such as civic duty, honesty, diligence, perseverance, respect, kindness, and independent-mindedness; which gives students step-by-step mastery of *procedural knowledge* in language arts and mathematics; which gives them step-by-step mastery of *content knowledge* in civics, science, the arts, and the humanities; and which holds students, teachers, schools, and parents accountable for acceptable progress in achieving these specific year-by-year goals. Every school, in short, should have the basic characteristics described in an earlier chapter:

> All teachers at our school have not only pedagogical training but also a detailed knowledge of the subject matter that they teach. We instill in all children an ethic of toleration, civility, orderliness, responsibility, and hard work. Our staff has agreed on a definite core of knowledge and skill that all children will attain *in each grade*. We make sure that every child learns this core, and gains the specific knowledge and skill needed to prosper at the next grade level, thus enabling knowledge to build upon knowledge. Our teachers continually confer with their colleagues about effective ways of stimulating children to learn and integrate this specific knowledge and skill. The specificity of our goals enables us to monitor children, and give focused attention where necessary. To this end, we provide parents with a detailed outline of the *specific* knowledge and skill goals for each grade, and we stay in constant touch with them regarding the child's progress. Through this knowledge-based approach, we make sure that *all* normal children perform at grade level, while, in addition, the most talented children are challenged to excel. Attaining this specific and well-integrated knowledge and skill gives our students pleasure in learning, as well as self-respect, and it ensures that they will enter the next grade ready and eager to learn more.

Since this emphasis on content and coherence requires a structur-   14
ing of ideas, and because ideas are slow to change, my colleagues and
I have been pursuing a school-by-school grassroots effort in which
the leadership of one group of parents or teachers, or of a single principal or superintendent, can revolutionize the ideas and practices of
an individual school. That school's success then sometimes encourages other schools to rethink their assumptions. This school-by-
school effort is slow, but it is at least an avenue that can be taken now,
without delay—the kind of initiative greatly facilitated by large-scale
policies that consciously liberate individual initiative, policies such
as "parental choice" and "charter schools," which give parents and
teachers the power to change their own individual schools, so long as
their students are trained to high standards of skill and knowledge.

It has taken nearly seventy years for Romantic progressivism to ex-   15
ercise virtually totalitarian intellectual dominion over not just schools
of education but a large percentage of policymakers and the general
public as well. Nothing truly effective in the way of large-scale policy
change—through federal, state, or local mechanisms—can be accomplished, no new power relationships can be forged, until there is a
change of mind by the general public—among whom I include two
and a half million teachers. Once that occurs, many different public
policies could be successful.

The strongest resistance to commonality in schooling may come   16
from a widespread fear of uniformity—the last bastion of misguided
Romanticism. It is said that common elements in the curriculum
would destroy our American essence, which is diversity. There is no
evidence whatever that this fear of uniformity, which is widespread
and often expressed, has any real-world foundation, or that a moiety
of commonality in the school curriculum will turn everyone into interchangeable automatons. To the extent that this antisameness sentiment has any concrete implication for the curriculum, it would seem
to be the current laissez-faire idea that if all schools and teachers
do their own thing, then the invisible hand of nature will cause our
children to be educated effectively, and thus ensure their individuality and diversity. The foundation for this curricular confidence (which
has in fact resulted in huge knowledge gaps, boring repetitions, and
glaring inequalities) would seem to be a Romantic faith in the watchful beneficence of nature, which "never did betray the heart that loved
her." It is an expression of the same optimistic naturalism which sup-
poses that the pace and quality of each child's scholarly attainments
are determined naturally, and will follow an innate course of development which should not be interfered with by external impositions of
drills and hard work.

Improving the effectiveness and fairness of education through en-   17
hancing both its content and its commonality has a more than educational significance. The improvement would, as everyone knows,

diminish the economic inequities within the nation. Nothing could be more important to our national well-being than overcoming those inequities, which have grown ever greater in recent decades. But something equally significant is at stake. Many observers have deplored the decline in civility in our public life, and with it the decline in our sense of community. The interethnic hostilities that have intensified among us recently, the development of an us-versus-them mentality in political life, the astonishing indifference to the condition of our children—all bespeak a decline in the communitarian spirit, which used to be a hallmark of what Patterson calls our "ecumenical national culture." Bringing our children closer to universal competence is important. But an equally important contribution of the truly common school would be the strengthening of universal communicability and a sense of community within the public sphere. In the long run, that could be the common school's most important contribution to preserving the fragile fabric of our democracy.

QUESTIONS FOR DISCUSSION

1   Why does Hirsch think that a common curriculum is necessary to the functioning of a democratic nation? What evidence does he present to support his point of view? Explain why you agree or disagree with him.

2   Hirsch also argues for a shared public culture. Do you agree with Hirsch on this point? Do you agree that a shared public culture is implied by the First Amendment?

3   How does Hirsch apply Bagley's research and Jefferson's ideas to support his argument for a core curriculum?

4   How does Hirsch believe that a common core curriculum could be established? Do you think his plan is realistic and could be implemented?

5   Does your college or local school district endorse a common curriculum? Why or why not? Explain why you agree or disagree with your college's position on a common curriculum

IDEAS FOR WRITING

1   Do you think that it would be possible or desirable to create a shared public culture in the United States? Who would help to create this public culture? Write an essay that explores your point of view.

2   Would you prefer to study and learn from a common core curriculum? Argue for or against a common core curriculum, using concrete evidence and examples to support each of your main points.

On Discipline

JOHN HOLT

*John Holt (1923–1985) has been a leader in the educational
reform movement. After graduating from Yale University, he taught
elementary school for fourteen years. He also taught at Harvard and
the University of California at Berkeley. Because Holt believed that
"learning is as natural as breathing," many of his books argue that
drills and other traditional structured classroom activities work
against the development of the child's creativity; therefore, he
suggested alternative forms of education. He was instrumental in
the growth of the alternative school movement and founded the
magazine* Growing Without Schooling. *His best-known books include*
How Children Fail *(1964),* How Children Learn *(1967),* What Do I
Do on Monday *(1970),* Escape from Childhood *(1974),* Instead of
Education *(1976), and* Teach Your Own *(1981). In the following
selection, excerpted from* Freedom and Beyond *(1972), Holt explains
why he believes that learning must be self-motivated and governed
by discipline, work, and love.*

"If we give children freedom how will they ever learn discipline?"   1
This is a common question—really a statement. When people talk
about their child "learning discipline," what is it that they really want
him to learn? Probably, most or all of the following:

1. Do what you're told without questioning or resisting, whenever
    I or any other authority tell you to do something.

2. Go on doing what you're told for as long as you're told. Never
    mind how dull, disagreeable, or pointless the task may seem. It's
    not for you to decide.

3. Do whatever we want you to do, *willingly*. Do it without even
    having to be told. Do what you're *expected* to do.

4. If you don't do these things you will be punished and you will
    deserve to be.

5. Accept your life without complaining even if you get very little if
    any of what you think you want, even if your life has not much
    joy, meaning, or satisfaction. That's what life is.

6. Take your medicine, your punishment, whatever the people
    above you do to you, without complaining or resisting.

7. Living this way is good for your soul and character.

Rather like the sermon the rich used to preach to the poor in   2
the early days of the Industrial Revolution: accept the station in life,
however humble, to which God has called you, and there meekly and

gratefully do your duty. This preaching still goes on, of course; the rich and powerful, for obvious reasons, always like to tell the poor and lowly about the virtues of duty, obedience, and hard work. Not long ago, after an evening meeting in a town of about 15,000 people, a man came up to me and said, "I run a bank here, and what I want to know is, if kids get the kind of education you're talking about, what are they going to do when I tell them that if they want to work in my bank they are going to have to get their hair cut and wear a suit and show up promptly at eight thirty in the morning?" I said, "Well, I suppose if a young person really wants to work in your bank, he will accept those conditions as part of the deal." He walked away looking dissatisfied. What I might have said to him, but didn't, was that if willingness to obey his orders was all he was looking for in his employees, he would probably not be in the banking business for long. Also, that perhaps the way he and many like him felt and behaved toward young people might have something to do with a problem others had told me about that day—that all the young people in the town were leaving as soon as they finished high school.

Some people who worry about discipline may not necessarily want   3
their children to believe *all* the ideas listed above. But most of the Americans who said in a recent nationwide poll that what they wanted above all else in schools was more discipline probably had all these ideas in mind. The Boston *Globe* reports that Vice-President Agnew recently said to a convention of farmers in Chicago, "I would think restoration of discipline and order ought to be a first priority— even ahead of curriculum—in the schools of this country." They add that his statement won Agnew louder applause than anything else he said to the farmers. What those farmers want is more coercion, more threats, more punishment, more fear. Above all, more fear. Make them afraid! They experience their own life as a kind of slavery, and this is what they want for their (and everyone else's) child, perhaps on the theory that if it's good enough for them it's good enough for him, if they can put up with it then by God he will, perhaps on the theory that nothing else is possible.

The word "discipline" has more and more important meanings   4
than just this. A child, in growing up, may meet and learn from three different kinds of disciplines. The first and most important is what we might call the Discipline of Nature or of Reality. When he is trying to do something real, if he does the wrong thing or doesn't do the right one, he doesn't get the result he wants. If he doesn't pile one block right on top of another, or tries to build on a slanting surface, his tower falls down. If he hits the wrong key, he hears the wrong note. If he doesn't hit the nail squarely on the head, it bends, and he has to pull it out and start with another. If he doesn't measure properly what he is trying to build, it won't open, close, fit, stand up, fly, float, whistle, or do what- ever he wants it to do. If he closes his eyes when he swings, he doesn't

hit the ball. A child meets this kind of discipline every time he tries to *do* something, which is why it is so important in school to give children more chances to do things, instead of just reading or listening to someone talk (or pretending to). This discipline is a great teacher. The learner never has to wait long for his answer; it usually comes quickly, often instantly. Also it is clear, and very often points toward the needed correction; from what happened he cannot only see that what he did was wrong, but also why, and what he needs to do instead. Finally, and most important, the giver of the answer, call it Nature, is impersonal, impartial, and indifferent. She does not give opinions, or make judgments; she cannot be wheedled, bullied, or fooled; she does not get angry or disappointed; she does not praise or blame; she does not remember past failures or hold grudges; with her one always gets a fresh start, this time is the one that counts.

The next discipline we might call the Discipline of Culture, of   5
Society, of What People Really Do. Man is a social, a cultural animal. Children sense around them this culture, this network of agreements, customs, habits, and rules binding the adults together. They want to understand it and be a part of it. They watch very carefully what people around them are doing and want to do the same. They want to do right, unless they become convinced they can't do right. Thus children rarely misbehave seriously in church, but sit as quietly as they can. The example of all those grownups is contagious. Some mysterious ritual is going on, and children, who like rituals, want to be part of it. In the same way, the little children that I see at concerts or operas, though they may fidget a little, or perhaps take a nap now and then, rarely make any disturbance. With all those grownups sitting there, neither moving nor talking, it is the most natural thing in the world to imitate them. Children who live among adults who are habitually courteous to each other, and to them, will soon learn to be courteous. Children who live surrounded by people who speak a certain way will speak that way, however much we may try to tell them that speaking that way is bad or wrong.

The third discipline is the one most people mean when they speak   6
of discipline—the Discipline of Superior Force, of sergeant to private, of "you do what I tell you or I'll make you wish you had." There is bound to be some of this in a child's life. Living as we do surrounded by things that can hurt children, or that children can hurt, we cannot avoid it. We can't afford to let a small child find out from experience the danger of playing in a busy street, or of fooling with the pots on the top of a stove, or of eating up the pills in the medicine cabinet. So, along with other precautions, we say to him, "Don't play in the street, or touch things on the stove, or go into the medicine cabinet, or I'll punish you." Between him and the danger too great for him to imagine we put a lesser danger, but one he can imagine and maybe therefore want to avoid. He can have no idea of what it would be like

to be hit by a car, but he can imagine being shouted at, or spanked, or sent to his room. He avoids these substitutes for the greater danger until he can understand it and avoid it for its own sake. But we ought to use this discipline only when it is necessary to protect life, health, safety, or well-being of people or other living creatures, to prevent destruction of things that people care about. We ought not to assume too long, as we usually do, that a child cannot understand the real nature of the danger from which we want to protect him. The sooner he avoids the danger, not to escape our punishment, but as a matter of good sense, the better. He can learn that faster than we think. In Mexico, for example, where people drive their cars with a good deal of spirit, I saw many children no older than five or four walking un-attended on the streets. They understood about cars, they knew what to do. A child whose life is full of threat and fear of punishment is locked into babyhood. There is no way for him to grow up, to learn to take responsibility for his life and acts. Most important of all, we should not assume that having to yield to the threat of our superior force is good for the child's character. It is never good for *anyone's* character. To bow to superior force makes us feel impotent and cowardly for not having had the strength or courage to resist. Worse, it makes us resentful and vengeful. We can hardly wait to make some-one yield. No, if we cannot always avoid using the Discipline of Superior Force, we should at least use it as seldom as we can.

There are places where all three disciplines overlap. Any very de-manding human activity combines in it the disciplines of Superior Force, of Culture, and of Nature. The novice will be told, "Do it this way, never mind asking why, just do it that way, that is the way we always do it." But it probably *is* just the way they always do it, and usually for the very good reason that it is a way that has been found to work. Think, for example, of ballet training. The student in a class is told to do this exercise, or that; to stand so; to do this or that with his head, arms, shoulders, abdomen, hips, legs, feet. He is constantly cor-rected. There is no argument. But behind these seemingly autocratic demands by the teacher lie many decades of custom and tradition, and behind that, the necessities of dancing itself. You cannot make the moves of classical ballet unless over many years you have ac-quired, and renewed every day, the needed strength and suppleness in scores of muscles and joints. Nor can you do the difficult motions, making them look easy, unless you have learned hundreds of easier ones first. Dance teachers may not always agree on all the details of teaching these strengths and skills. But no novice could learn them all by himself. You could not go for a night or two to watch the ballet and then, without any other knowledge at all, teach yourself how to do it. In the same way, you would be unlikely to learn any complicated human activity without drawing heavily on the experience of those who know it better. But the point is that the authority of these experts or teachers stems from, grows out of their greater competence and experience, the fact that what they do *works*, not the fact that they happen to be the teacher and as such have the power to kick a student out of the class. And the further point is that children are always and everywhere attracted to that competence, and ready and eager to submit themselves to a discipline that grows out of it. We hear constantly that children will never do anything unless compelled to by bribes or threats. But in their private lives, or in extracurricular activities in school, in sports, music, drama, art, running a newspaper, and so on, they often submit themselves willingly and wholeheartedly to very intense disciplines, simply because they want to learn to do a given thing well. Our Little-Napoleon football coaches, of whom we have too many and hear far too much, blind us to the fact that millions of children work hard every year getting better at sports and games without coaches barking and yelling at them.

Some experts, in writing about discipline, try to equate and lump   8
together what I have called the Discipline of Nature and the Discipline of Superior Force. They say that when we tell a child to do something, and punish him if he does not, we are teaching him to understand the natural consequences of his acts. In a widely praised book one expert gave this typical advice. If your child comes home late to dinner, tell him that he can't have any dinner, and he will soon learn the natural consequences of being late and coming home on time. The example is confused, foolish, and wrong. Being denied any dinner can be called a "natural" consequence of coming home late only in the sense that anything and everything that happens is a part of reality and hence can be called "natural." One might as easily say that being flogged was also a "natural" consequence of being late. In fact, getting no dinner is not a natural consequence of being late at all, but a purely arbitrary one imposed by the parents. The *natural* consequence of coming home late to dinner might be that your dinner would be cold, or that you would have to eat much or all of it alone, or that you would have to clear your place when you had finished and wash your dishes yourself. Not getting any dinner might be a natural consequence of coming home *unexpectedly*, so that nothing was prepared for you. But it is not a natural consequence of being late. It is punishment pure and simple. As such, it might be effective, and it might not. The child might learn the lesson. Or he might think bitterly, "Boy, some family, you come home late and even though you've got your dinner all cooked, just sitting out there in the kitchen, they won't let you eat it, they'd rather throw the food away, waste it, like they're always telling you not to do, just to make you go to bed hungry and teach you a lesson. I'll show them. I'll get my food somewhere else and come home late every night. I won't come home at all." Punishers always tell the punished that their punishments are the natural consequences of their acts. Not so. They are the result of a choice which the punishers,

or the authority they represent, have forced on the punished. The choice may be a wise and just one, or it may not; in either case, it is imposed, not natural.

1 How does Holt's breakdown of discipline into three categories help you to understand the concept of discipline better?

2 How do Holt's examples clarify his presentation of the types of discipline?

3 How does Holt apply his theory of meaningful discipline to explain the failure of schools to educate children who have talent and ability?

4 Working with a small group of your classmates, develop from your own life experiences several examples of each form of discipline that Holt explains and write a definition of discipline. Share your group's examples and definition with the class as a whole.

1 Write an argument that supports or refutes Holt's theory about how children learn most effectively

2 Write an extended definition of discipline. Like Holt, include examples to show how discipline has helped you to achieve your goals and/or find happiness.

CONNECTONS: TOPICS FOR THOUGHT, RESEARCH, AND WRITING

1   Imagine a typical writing classroom in the year 2010. What topics and writers might be included in the curriculum? What role might technology, such as computers, the Internet, and multimedia, play in the classroom? Will the class be student-centered, teacher-centered, or computer-centered?

2   Write an essay that presents what you have learned—from selections in this anthology and from your own experiences—about an aspect of education, such as the role of the teacher, group work, and classroom dynamics in promoting effective learning.

3   Write an essay that focuses on the role of cultural and linguistic diversity and multiculturalism in education. Consider the opinions of writers such as Angelou, Rodriguez, and hooks. You can do further research on the issued and then present you own conclusions.

4   Reflect on the approach of several remarkable teachers, including some of those profiled in this book as well as teachers you have encountered personally: these might include a spiritual leader, a professor, a coach or exercise instructor, an art or music teacher, a counselor, a parent, or even a good friend. Then write a paper discussing each one's methods; develop comparisons and contrasts. Draw your own conclusions about how both formal and informal "teachers" help one to learn.

5   Write an argument that supports or refutes the concept of a core curriculum.

6   Write an imaginary dialogue between two of the writers in this anthology on a controversial educational issue, such as bilingual education, the use of technology, or a standardized curriculum.

7   After considering the different theories about the learning process of writers such as Holt or Gardner, write an essay that presents your theory of how learning takes place. Refer to your own experiences as well as to the ideas of writers in this anthology to support your point of view.

8   Watch one or more current films or videos that explore an issue related to education. Choices might include *The Miracle Worker*, *Hoop Dreams*, *Dead Poets' Society*, *To Stand and Deliver*, *Dangerous Minds*, or *Mr. Holland's Opus*. Then write a paper in which you show how the film(s) develop(s) several of the issues presented in particular reading selections in this anthology.

Acknowledgments (*continued*)

John Holt, "On Discipline" from *Freedom and Beyond*. Reprinted by permission of Holt Associates: Freedom and Beyond (Boynton/Cook Publishers. A subsidiary of Greenwood Publishing Group, Portsmouth, NH, 1995, 1972).

bell hooks, "Keeping Close to Home: Class and Education." Reprinted, from *Talking Back: Thinking Feminist, Thinking Black,* with permission from the publisher, South End Press, 116 Saint Botolph Street, Boston, MA 02115. Copyright © 1989.

Maxine Hong Kingston, "The Silent Girl" from *Woman Warrior*. Copyright © 1975, 1976 by Maxine Hong Kingston. Reprinted by permission of Alfred A. Knopf Inc.

Jonathan Kozol, "Corla Hawkins" from *Savage Inequalities*. Copyright © 1991 by Jonathan Kozol. Reprinted by permission of Crown Publishers, Inc.

Richard Rodriguez, "Private and Public Language" from *Hunger of Memory*. Reprinted by permission of David R. Godine, Publisher, Inc. Copyright © 1982 by Richard Rodriguez.

Mike Rose, excerpt from *Possible Lives: The Promise of Public Education in America*. Copyright © 1995 by Mike Rose. Reprinted by permission of Houghton Mifflin Company. All rights reserved.

Amy Tan, "Mother Tongue." Copyright © 1990 by Amy Tan. First appeared in *The Threepenny Review*. Reprinted by permission of Amy Tan and the Sandra Dijkstra Literary Agency.

Deborah Tannen, "Teachers' Classroom Strategies Should Recognize That Men and Women Use Language Differently." 1991 copyright Deborah Tannen. Reprinted by permission.